Double Entry Bookkeeping

Or

Dear Cilla

The Easy Way to Debit and Credit all the way to Trial Balance

With an addendum on how to calculate the value of the firm's economic rent from the Trial Balance

By

TIM WALSHAW

ISBN: 978-0-9876113-2-1

Previous related publication by Tim Walshaw:
Increasing Returns to Scale*: *A Simple Way to Make Good Investments, and Not Bad Investments, When Investing in Company Shares. Economic Rents, the Hidden Profit: How to Find Safe Companies to Invest In. Taxing Economic Rents.

DEDICATED

TO

THE LATE CILLA BLACK
ENTERTAINER

THE PATRON SAINT OF ALL BOOKKEEPERS

Index

Introduction

This book goes as far as the Trial Balance, and deriving a simple Profit and Loss Statement and Balance Sheet from this Trial Balance. There is also an Addendum on how to estimate the Economic Rent earned by the firm from this information.

The reason for stopping this book at the Trial Balance is that at this point the duties of the Accountant takes over. That is how accounting is taught. The average Accountant usually has only a reduced understanding of bookkeeping.

The aim of this book is to give the reader a thorough understanding of the basics of Double Entry Bookkeeping, and how to do it. It supplies a simple set of mnemonics, which once memorized, will make all those trick questions in bookkeeping exams a breeze. You will need to know just two sets of information:- whether you are increasing or decreasing the value of the account; and, what of four categories of accounts is it – Asset, Liability, Income or Expenditure. Once you have the answer these two required sets of information, the process will be automatic and be correct every time.

The vital study of Double Entry Bookkeeping suffers from at least three major handicaps. The subject is ignored by the vast majority of the population, even though for their own sakes they should be full conversant with the technique. Secondly, many of those taught, and indeed many of accountants, practitioners and bookkeepers, do not fully understand the double entry technique. Nowadays they resort to computerized bookkeeping programs, providing a black box for the accounts, and many bookkeepers are no more than computer key pushers working on a single-entry accounting system. And finally, and this is the ultimate affront, professional accountants look down on bookkeeping and feel that their professional services only start when the trial balance has been completed. From that point forward they can fiddle with asset valuations and transaction values and produce the profit figure desired! As a consequence, most if not all accounting courses at the tertiary level tend to jump over, skate over, or ignore bookkeeping, and go straight to the "interesting" subject of how to manipulate asset values through depreciation, asset appreciation or more arcane methods such as accrual accounting, so that they can get the profit figure they want!

Yet in the past, a good knowledge of double entry bookkeeping was the source of vast fortunes. The Medicis, who created the vast Renaissance banking fortune, were masters of double entry bookkeeping. Roll forward a few centuries, and David Rockefeller attributed the start of his vast wealth to the good fortune of learning double entry bookkeeping as a youth.

You will benefit vastly from learning the basics of double entry booking. It is not complicated and confusing. It is not boring. In fact the way I teach it, it is fun. You don't need a computer. Indeed, you don't even need expensive accounting books. Those heavy ledgers went out a century ago. As long as you are clear, neat, logical, and make an effort to create the correct layout, you can use any set of blank or lined paper books.

However, you do need books to write in. Loose sheets of paper, or typed cards, even those recommended by some proprietary accounting systems with carbon paper inserts, are not recommended. The pages must be bound and locked into place. A permanent record. That is why they are called books and the process is called bookkeeping. In fact, in my opinion this requirement is superior to using computers, where the electronic data is not permanent, or even the computers' predecessors, the typed ledger cards. Figures can go missing forever. Maybe I am excessively old fashioned. But in this book you will learn bookkeeping using books. Pages that cannot go missing. If and when you go onto more technologically advanced methods, keep the telephone number of your auditor handy. The "missing figures that balance" scam is a perennial problem and event.

This book has a different approach to most textbooks on this subject. They start by saying "Imagine you are setting up a business ABC" and then go on to describe all the books and accounts you need. Pretty soon all students have been taught this method go blaaaah! They quickly begin to ask the question "Why?" and become dissatisfied and restive. "Just do this" is not enough.

A fundamental understanding of the reason for the required methodology is necessary. The students need to be comfortable that the proposed accounting method is needed, and it is not taught just so the student can pass exams and obtain a job. For this reason I start by discussing alternative bookkeeping methods that have been tried and point out their flaws, and why double entry bookkeeping is not only better, but absolutely essential.

As an aside, it is my impression that if you ask accountants why double-entry bookkeeping is superior to single entry bookkeeping, the vast majority of accountants have absolutely no idea. This is the reason why there has been an almost complete takeover by computerized bookkeeping methods, that are, let's face it, little more than glorified single-entry bookkeeping methods, regardless of what goes on inside them. When the knowledge spreads about how easy it is to defraud even the most sophisticated computerized single-entry system, it will be a major shock to the business community, both big and small.

As you go through this book you will probably think that the method described, using hand ledgers and 'strike-outs', is excessively old fashioned in this computerized age. But you will come to realize that the method described is the correct method, and it can be adapted, once you understand it, to modern technology. The purpose of the book is to teach you the fundamentals of double entry bookkeeping. You can adapt this knowledge to modern equipment.

More importantly, you can raise questions regarding your 'modern' bookkeeping system – by asking does it do this or that? As a matter of fact, the vast majority of modern bookkeeping systems take short-cuts, are not actually double entry bookkeeping as described in detail in this book, but are single-entry databases, and are very unsafe. To show my knowledge of computerized bookkeeping packages, I will tell you now that software can be downloaded from the 'dark web' that can rob you blind without you knowing it. It is easy to change a single entry in a database and nobody will be the wiser. You can tell from the length of time these accounting packages take to give you a trial balance, that they have to reconstruct all the ledger pages from the database before they can do it!

Don't trust computerized bookkeeping. Use this book to learn double entry bookkeeping from the first steps. You will then know how to check if your computerized bookkeeping system is not actually robbing you.

Chapter 1

The History of Double Entry Bookkeeping

Many people regard history as a waste of time. But history is recounting experience. And the accounting experience before double entry bookkeeping came along was very bad. It kept firms small. Basically a tiny group you could trust. Your family, or a couple of partners and a trusted clerk. Why? In a few words, single entry bookkeeping. There was no way to double check that you had added up the figures correctly, or indeed you had included everything. No small problem when Roman numerals were used in the books. No firm could expand past a small size. Large estates and government transactions were open to large-scale fraud.

Indeed such was the extent of this problem that the English Treasury devised a primitive form of a spreadsheet - a large table cloth divided into black and white squares as in a chess board. As a consequence, the English Treasury gained the name the "Exchequer". I am not going to go into an explanation how the system worked here. Suffice to say, as your spreadsheet accounting system is today, it is not a perfect form of accounting, though it can catch some basic errors.

It is likely that double entry bookkeeping originally started in India (as well as the so called Arabic numbering system) some two thousand years ago. The 'Bania' merchants used a form of double entry called 'bahi-kahatia'. This spread to the Arabic world along with Indian numbers. It is certain that double-entry bookkeeping was used since the ninth century by the Arabs operating in North Africa before being taken up by European traders. It is recorded that in AD 976 the scholars Al Khawarizmy and Al Mazendarany described a method recording receipts on the right-hand page and payments on the left-hand page, a precursor to double-entry bookkeeping, and equivalent to a modern-day Journal.

The earliest known use of double entry accounting, a surviving fragment, is the ledger of a Florentine bank dated 1211. It uses Roman numerals, but otherwise shows the essential features of a double entry account, debtors and creditors. More complete records date from around 1300, with the accounts of the Florentine merchants Rinieri Fini and Brothers, and Giovanni Farolfi & Co. These, as described by the accounting historian G.A. Lee, show the essential features of double entry accounts. In the words of Jane Gleeson-White, author of the book 'Double Entry', these essential features are:

- First, the idea of a proprietor or business partnership as an accounting entity whose books record its financial relationships with others.
- Second, its entries are made in a single monetary unit that can be added together. Third, it relates the following oppositions: increases and decreases in

physical holdings of cash or goods; increases and decreases in debts by or to other individuals and entities; and increases and decreases in the business's own assets and liabilities.
- Fourth, owners' equity is shown as the net of the assets and liabilities.
- Fifth, profit is understood to be the net increase in the owner's equity (and loss the net decrease).
- Sixth, the profit or loss is measured over a clearly defined accounting period.

However, the major influence for the introduction of double entry bookkeeping was a book on mathematics written one hundred years later, that in part, along with a lot of other mathematical information, gave a simple set of rules and practical advice on how to conduct double entry bookkeeping. The author was Luca Bartolomeo de Pacioli. The book was called *Summa de arithmetica, geometria et proportiioni et proportionalita*, the last part only of which was the description of double entry bookkeeping *Particularis de computis et scripturis* ('Particulars of Reckonings and Writings'), published in 1494 in Venice.

Why Pacioli ended his book with a section on bookkeeping is not possible to discover. It is likely Pacioli wanted to produce a best seller, and included anything that would of likely interest to the wealthy merchants of Venice of the day. This is the era when both the Medieval and Renaissance periods had finished; moveable type printing had been used for 40 years; and Columbus had sailed to America and Vasco de Gama to India. I won't describe Pacioli's varied life as a travelling scholar, a friend of among others of Leonardo do Vinci, except to mention he was born about 1440 in the town of Sansepolcro, north Rome, started life as a travelling lecturer in arithmetic and Arabic numerals, travelled to many towns including Venice, became a Professor of Mathematics at the Universities of Rome and Milan, and wrote and published several books on mathematics.

Why did Pacioli write the *Summa de arithmetica, geometria et proportiioni et proportionalita*? For a start, Pacioli was a habitual author. He had written a dozen books on mathematics, printed and sold widely. In the standards of the day he was a best-selling author. But he probably had an additional reason for including the section on bookkeeping *Particularis de computis et scripturis* . He felt that a practical description of how to do double entry bookkeeping in the 'Venetian style' was a necessity for all merchants and businessmen. In his words, if a merchant follows the system Pacioli sets out, 'then he will always know all about his business and will know exactly whether his business goes well or not. Therefore the proverb: If you are in business, and do not know about it, your money will go like flies – That is, you will lose it.'

Pacioli's instructions on double entry bookkeeping were only the latter part of the book. Nonetheless, this section of this part of the book was re-printed many times by other authors, translated, and was used to widely spread the knowledge of double entry bookkeeping. Within 100 years this section had been reprinted many times in several languages. A German version was printed in Nurembourg in 1537. Domenico Manzoni published an expanded Italian version in 1540 in Venice, including many examples in the text. The first Dutch version was published in 1543 by Jan Ympyn Christoffels *New instruction and demonstration of the praised art of ciphering.* This was translated into English. The earliest known English work is in 1543 by Hugh Oldcastle *A profitable treatyce called the Instrument or Boke to learne to knowe the good order of kepying of the famous reconynge called in Latyn Dare and Habere and in Englyshe Debitor and Creditor.*

It would be nice to say that double entry bookkeeping spread rapidly after that, but in actual fact the spread was slow. Single entry or very primitive bookkeeping was the norm well into the start of the Industrial Revolution right at the start of the Nineteenth Century.

Pacioli's instructions were succinct. After starting the books with an invocation to God (a usual and necessary requirement in those days – profit from trade in those days was frowned on by the Church), he instructed the bookkeeper to start with a general record book, which he called a 'Memorandum' book. All transactions, both buy and sell, were entered in this book in date order of the transaction, with full and complete details including the amount. This book was necessary as the ultimate source of information. From this book, in order, all other entries were made in all the other books Pacioli described.

The next book Pacioli described was the 'Journal'. All the transactions were entered in date order from the Memorandum book on a single line, and each entry carried the amount, a transaction or Journal number and date. But this time the transactions are divided into two parts, "Per" and "A" on the same line, with the "Per" and "A" referring to two different accounts, divided by a double slash //. (Yes, budding accountants will know that the bookkeeping process with its Debits and Credits has transmigrated to the modern Journal, but I am describing Pacioli's day). A simple enough exercise, and most traders in those days followed this routine, if they kept records at all.

For example, in Pacioli's day, the merchant could have bought 1000 Ducats of nutmegs, drawing 1000 Ducats from his capital. The convention in those days was to write in the Journal on one line "Per nutmegs//A capital 1000". Note that two Accounts are now mentioned – Nutmegs, and Capital. Per means that you are increasing the value of that Account, A means that you are decreasing the value of that Account, both by the same stated amount.

When the nutmegs are sold for 1500 Ducats, say, the procedure would be to write in the Journal "Per capital//A nutmegs 1500".

Pacioli then goes into an explanation for the important words Debit and Credit. In Latin 'Debere' means to owe, and ' Credere', to believe. He explained that the term *debiti* means what is owed to me. *Crediti* means what is owed by me. If nobody believed in your good name, Credere, nobody would lend you money. Pacioli explained that the word of a good merchant is a substitute for capital. "… many without capital of their own, but whose credit is good, carry on big transactions and by means of their credit, which they faithfully kept, became very wealthy. In the great republics nothing was considered superior to the word of a good merchant."

From here Pacioli described the next account book – the Ledger, and the process of entering transactions into the Ledger. The Ledger was described by Pacioli as a large volume with many numbered pages, each page for a different Account., and each page had the title of that Account at its head. At the start of the Ledger there was inserted an Index for all the Accounts referring to different page numbers, so that the bookkeeper could quickly find the required Account in the Ledger.

Each Ledger page had a standard layout. There were five columns. In Pacioli's day the layout was much the same as today, although there have since been variations. The first column related to the date of the transaction. The next column related to the number of the transaction in the Journal, referred to as the 'Journal Number'. This number is necessary for Audits and error detection. The next column, a relatively wider one, has an account name written in it. But this account name is not the name of the account you are writing into, but the name of another account. (Which one will be described in a minute). The final two columns have the names 'Debit' and 'Credit'. By convention the Debit column is to the left of the Credit column.

The instructions by Pacioli were clear. First, take each recently completed Journal entry in order of entry. Turn to the Account name shown on the Journal. Then enter the date of the transaction in the first column, and the number of the transaction in the Journal in the next column.

Now we come to the core of the process, *double entry.*

Pacioli insists on a second entry for each transaction, on another Account page. Furthermore, for every Debit entry a Credit entry must be made, and for every Credit entry a Debit entry must be made. The major reasons for performing double entry, according to Pacioli, were threefold; error detection, prevention of fraud, and the wonderful invention, the Trial Balance, from which the Balance Sheet and Profit and Loss Statement can be obtained directly.

You cannot obtain a Trial Balance from Single Entry. That is the overriding reason why Double Entry is preferable to Single Entry. And a Trial Balance is vital for finding your current financial position. More of this later.

In Pacioli's day, if a merchant did not use Double Entry Bookkeeping, the merchant had only a rough idea if he was making a profit, or indeed if he was solvent. Many merchants, as they do today, continued to trade if they were insolvent. Some survived. Some did not. Their demise, as Shakespeare described in "The Merchant of Venice" was often sudden and painful.

Since Pacioli's day there have been developments in accounting. The major one was in the mid-Nineteenth Century, after the so-called "Railway Crisis", when there was a crash in railway shares in Britain, leading to the introduction of the depreciation of assets. Accounting jumped from mere bookkeeping to more complex adjustments to the accounts aimed at producing what was felt to be a "true and fair" picture of the entity's financial position.

My hope is that one day all published company accounts should show a Trial Balance as well, developed from the accounting position of all the Ledgers on a single day, together with a Balance Sheet and Profit and Loss Statement drawn from that Trial Balance. These can then be compared with the published Balance Sheet and Profit and Loss Statement prepared by the Company Accountants, with clear explanations of the differences in the figures. You would be amazed at the amount of fraud and manipulation this would prevent.

LIMITATIONS OF TRIAL BALANCE

In order of frequency and importance.

- ERRORS OF OMISSION – when a transaction is completely omitted from the accounting records.
- COMPENSATING ERRORS – errors that cancel each other out on the Debit and Credit side. They may be multiple unrelated errors that would individually lead to an imbalance.
- ERROR OF COMMISSION – when the entries are made for the correct amount in both the Debit and Credit accounts, but one or more entries are posted to the wrong account.
- ERROR OF REVERSAL – when entries are made to the correct accounts, but Debits are posted as Credits, and vice versa.
- ERROR OF ORIGINAL ENTRY – when both sides of the transaction include the wrong amount.

As will be described shortly, if the accounting system included the use of the so-called Memorandum, most of these errors and omissions, except possibly Errors of Reversal, would be obviated, and would not occur at all. Certainly the current standard methods of deliberate fraud would be entirely eliminated.

While a Trial Balance can stand on its own, and any moderately well-informed person can obtain useful information from it, it can also be divided into two parts, and an Income Statement and Balance Sheet can be derived from each part. This procedure will be described later in this book.

CHAPTER 2

THE ADVANTAGES OF DOUBLE ENTRY BOOKEEPING

Many, if not most textbooks do not discuss at all the advantages of double entry bookkeeping over single entry bookkeeping. They usually just jump straight into it. "We now set up the accounts of business ABC", they say. The authors of these treatises don't hear the reader's question "Why should I bother? Why should I double my accounting costs?"

THE DISADVANTAGES OF SINGLE ENTRY BOOKKEEPING

Why bother with anything more complicated? Pacioli gave the reasons, and these reasons are rarely if ever described by modern textbooks on bookkeeping that jump straight into a description of double-entry, without describing its advantage over single entry. It is this:

1. Single entry cannot easily keep track of what you borrow and lend (vital for banking).
2. Single entry cannot easily keep track of the value of stocks and assets, and the net value of your business.
3. Error detection and fraud prevention in double entry is much easier, and virtually impossible in single entry.
4. You can't do a Trial Balance using single entry bookkeeping.
5. The construction of a balance sheet is much easier with double entry, as you go straight from a Trial Balance, though with single entry you may still do a simple cash profit and loss.

Furthermore, later writers point out that only double entry can show the individual profit figures for each line of merchandise, if you have separate accounts for these items of merchandise, while single entry can only show the total profit figure for each business. This is the starting point of the vast subject of cost accounting that lies at the core of modern industry.

The single overriding reason why using double entry is preferable to single entry is that you cannot derive a trial balance using single entry. You can jog along with the above reasons 1, 2 and 3 with single entry (though you will quickly go off the rails). Without a trial balance a businessman, as Pacioli said, "will suffer many sleepless nights and many worries". You will be lost.

Employee honesty

The basic need for accounting beyond a single person business is the issue of employee honesty. Let's face it, a high proportion of potential employees are dishonest and will steal from you if given an opportunity. If you are not willing to face that fact, you will certainly be robbed blind. In their 2016 "Report to the Nation on Occupational Fraud and Abuse", the Association of Certified Fraud Examiners (ACFE) reports that small businesses on average suffer a loss of $180,000 due to, face it, *stealing*, due to a lack of basic accounting controls and an excessive degree of misplaced trust.

On the psychology of individuals, I shall make a very painful observation about human psychology. I have found that many psychologists have the opinion, and I have confirmed this from my own experience, that around 20 per cent of the population is congenitally dishonest. That is, this 20 per cent would not hesitate to steal any amount, large or small, if there is a high probability that they would not be caught, or if caught, punished. Having an accounting system relying solely on a person's honesty is foolish and open to larceny.

Patricia Shaefer who wrote the web blog "Are employees stealing from you? Tips to prevent employee theft" (http://www.businessknowhow.com/manage/employee-theft.htm) refers to the 10-10-80 rule. 10 percent steal at any opportunity (*regardless of whether they are likely to be caught or not*). 10 per cent will never steal no matter what. The other 80 percent of employees will go either way depending on how they will rationalize a particular opportunity. Painful!

I recommend reading her blog, as it covers no less than 14 key ways to prevent employee theft.

The double entry system, if properly implemented, requires double-checking by at least two persons at every step of the way. (On this, I refer to the modern computerized systems, many of which use a single person to make *all* entries. These have become horror stories of fraud. If you use one of those computerized systems, use two persons, one to make the Debit entries and one to make the Credit entries, so that part at least is double-checked).

Pacioli extols double entry bookkeeping for the peace of mind it gives to a merchant. "Double entry is very essential to merchants, because without making the entries systematically it would be impossible to conduct their business, for they would have no rest and their minds be always troubled." That alone according to Pacioli is one of the most important reason for using a double entry accounting system, and who can deny that?

CHAPTER 3

INVENTORY AND CAPITAL STOCK

While I stated at the beginning that I would not mention "Starting business ABC", businesses do not jump into existence. They all start with some capital, and with some cash and assets. This book was written for such start-ups as well as pre-existing operating businesses. But in either case, to start a double entry bookkeeping system, you need to do a survey of what the business owns and what it owes *at a particular point in time*. Such as one day. You need to make an inventory.

According to Pacioli, the merchant when he starts the business, 'must always put down on a sheet of paper or in a separate book whatever he has in the world, personal property or real estate, beginning with the things that are most valuable and most likely to be lost, such as cash, jewels, silver,etc.' Completed in one day 'otherwise there will be trouble in the future management of the business'.

The initial inventory may appear in total in the "Memorandum" to be discussed in the next chapter, and from there transferred to the "Journal", discussed in further chapters. Pacioli recommends for 15th Century Italy to keep the inventory details secret in a separate book, and only use the total value.

And yes, as you may be aware, the inventory in modern firms needs to be rechecked and noted once a year, as changes in inventory values appear both in the Balance Sheet and Profit and Loss Statement. It is often the duty of the bookkeeper to conduct regular inventory valuations. So, don't neglect taking an inventory right at the very start, and at regular intervals. Your accounting system rests on the Inventory and Capital values.

There are standard methods to conduct an annual inventory. I won't discuss them here. Follow them. They are well tried. For an ongoing firm, you will encounter 'wastage' – theft. If it gets excessive employ audit firms who specialize in this area. (Ignore the protestations of your current auditors who are obviously not up to this task). Pilfering MUST be stamped on, or employees very rapidly see it as a right to pilfer.

As for fixed capital assets, revaluing capital assets is an arcane business. This is really the area for the accountant. Normally a bookkeeper is not involved in this, and does not put revalued assets into a Trial Balance, but uses the starting figures in the accounts.

CHAPTER 4

THE MEMORANDUM

My early background in England had some connection to a few large country estates. The owners of these estates were always short of money. I used to do back of the envelope calculations (even then I was an incipient economist) and worked out that these estate owners always seemed to receive income much less than they should. These estates were run by people called agents, whose position was semi-hereditary and who lived in large houses and lived very well indeed. Yes, the books were audited. The books always balanced. Nothing was wrong. Yet the estate income never seemed to be what it should be. "I am sorry Your Grace…."

I have also met wealthy people called "trust funders". They relied on income from trusts set up by their parents or grandparents. If you looked at their assets, their income never seemed to match a decent rate of return. They just kept getting poorer. Yet the people who actually ran the trust funds seemed to be getting richer. Yes, the trust fund was audited. The books balanced. "I am sorry, there were losses…."

It seemed that there was a steady bleeding of the income….

Back in 1500 Pacioli was onto to this, and started his accounting system with something called a *Memoriale*, now called the "Memorandum Book", a list of all transactions, buy and sell, as they occurred. Nowadays modern-day accountants jump straight to the Journal. They do not use a Memorandum Book. If His Grace and all the trust funders had used a Memorandum, otherwise known as a Day Book, or a Waste Book, as they are sometimes called, they would be considerably and consistently richer. Why?

From the practical accounting point of view, I believe the Memorandum is by far the most important book of accounts. It is also the simplest. But this activity is the most neglected.

I shall describe the standard accounting system, starting with the Memorandum. Never heard of it? I shall explain.

STEPS IN DOUBLE ENTRY BOOKEEPING

1. MEMORANDUM
2. JOURNAL
3. LEDGER
4. BANK RECONCILIATION
5. TRIAL BALANCE
6. BALANCE SHEET AND PROFIT AND LOSS

Descriptions of double entry bookkeeping start off with the Memorandum. This is nowadays sometimes called a "Day Book", or "Waste Book". This is the modern name for Pacioli's '*Memoriale*'. If you prefer to use the term Waste Book or Day Book, why not? But, unfortunately, nowadays this Waste Book or Memorandum Book is not often used, and bookkeepers go straight to the next book up the hierarchy, the Journal. However, in early Medieval times, and even in deciphered texts from ancient Ur, the Memorandum was what was used as the primary entry.

Some fifty or a hundred years ago, the Day Book, as it was then called, was a standard part of the operations of most small businesses. In it, there was no reference to Debits and Credits, and it contained a full description of each sale and purchase activity in date order. The usual methodology back then was often to use it as a form of Journal, and make entries straight from it into the Ledger. The Ledger contained the first mention of Debits and Credits.

Over the intervening years bookkeeping methodology has evolved, and keeps evolving. The Day Book or the Memorandum has largely disappeared, and entries are made from the source documents directly into the Journal complete with Debits and Credits. Indeed, with modern computerized accounting, all reference to the Journal also has largely disappeared. I shudder to think what goes on in these computerized systems. There appears to be direct entry into something that calls itself a Ledger, actually some form of single entry database. I fear many computerized systems are little more than glorified single-entry systems, open to the widest ranging frauds.

A Memorandum is as Pacioli described 'a book in which the merchant shall put down all his transactions, small or big, as they take place, day by day, hour by hour'. In this book the merchant must record the details of 'everything that he sells or buys, and every other transaction without leaving out a jot; who, what, where, mentioning everything to make it full as clear…' Pacioli devotes two chapters detailing what should go in the *Memoriale*, and this list is very useful for historians to understand what

Venetian merchants traded, from gold Ducats to linen, pepper and skins. The clear inference from the amount of detail recorded in the *Memoriale* is that Pacioli accorded it a very high level of importance. Further, if the Merchant is away on his travels and the *Memoriale* is maintained by his servants, Pacioli seems to infer that the *Memoriale* is maintained or double-checked by *two* servants.

So what is this *Memoriale* or Memorandum? It is a list, describing in detail all purchases and sales, all borrowing and lending, one after the other, in date order. It is a list of all transactions over time.

Should you use a Memorandum? Always. Yes, there is significant extra cost. For a large firm it would require a major department to record all the details, starting with the initial transactions. But as I shall explain, using a Memorandum system saves yourself or the firm major invisible losses and trouble.

Sad to say, in modern accounting procedures, as I said, the Memorandum has been frequently done away with. The bookkeeping system jumps straight from 'Documents' to the Journal. Documents are the source documents issued by the firm. Receipts, invoices, cash register slips, checks and check butts, bank deposit forms, payment vouchers, purchase orders, credit notes, internal memos, petty cash vouchers, the myriad pieces of paper that make up a business' operations. Many business' have a system where these individual pieces of paper move up to be directly recorded in the Journal, or there is an electronic system which is supposed to update the Journal directly when the documents are issued.

Unfortunately, the procedure to enter the Journal straight from the individual documents is sometimes disastrous, for the simple reason that *if* the transaction is **not** *initially recorded* in the bookkeeping system the money can easily be diverted into an employee's pocket, and this person is rarely caught. And this frequently happens. The books still balance, but profits are less.

For instance, a major fraud is the 'missing invoice scam'. Say the record for invoices sent to customers for goods just disappear, not recorded, and the payment received for them disappears down the track. There is no evidence that the money is missing. The books still balance. This hole in the accounting system has been a major problem for some very large companies for over a century. If there is a system to directly record all documents issued, holus bolus, into a Memorandum, and from *thence* into a Journal, with *double checks* back to the Memorandum from the Journal, this whole problem is largely obviated.

You think your business is too big to bother with this? I could tell you stories of a major car manufacturing company that lost money from car orders worth millions for nearly a century, just because some invoices were not recorded at this point, the weak point of all accounting systems. (The payments received for these invoices sent to the customer but not recorded were just diverted. These accounting positions in this company became valuable hereditary roles!) If nothing gets recorded, the transaction does not exist, and the books balance. Your profits are just lower!!!!

An example of a Memorandum is shown here:

MEMORANDUM (Example)

Date	Entry	Journal number
25 July 12	Issued receipts no 541 to 551 to Ollie Ayrton, Sue Rabbidge, James Chatfield, Annie Ajmera, James Burston, Lutana McLeod, Brendon Black, Tim Walshaw, For Membership Dues $54 cash each.	123
26 July12	Deposited $540 at Bank. Bank receipts $540. Westfield Bank receipt no 214870.	124
	(Stick all receipts and documents in ring folder. Original records must be kept 7 years).	
27 July12	Purchased three trophies for speaking contest. $20 each. Paid check no 8476 99. $60. Carter Trophies receipt no 6174.	125
30 July12	Purchased refreshments for contest. I Paid cash. $50. Hellas Club receipt no 5480.	126
30 July 12	Check refund for cash paid for refreshments. $50. Check no 847 00.	126
1 Aug 12	Received Entrance fees for contest. $5 each. $150.	127
2 Aug 12	Deposited $150 at Bank. Bank receipts $150. Westfield Bank receipt no 214871.	128
3 Aug 12	Club purchase on 30 day credit from District Supplies 20 manual at $4 each. $80	129
10 Aug 12	Sold a Manual on Credit to member Brendon Black $5	130
24 Aug 12	Brendon Black repays Club $5 for Manual, cash	131
30 Aug 12	Account at District Supplies is paid by bank check $80	132

I am using as an example the accounts of a debating club. The reason for this that as the club has no depreciable assets or long-term borrowings, its accounts are very simple. Even so the number of transactions soon add up. It is necessary to complete all transactions without delay!

Note that it is assumed that prior to the start of operations, or at the beginning of the year, there has been a careful survey of all the Club's physical assets, and the value of these appear in the accounts and the balance sheet at the beginning of the year.

The essential features of the Memorandum are the date column on the left, and a wider description column in the middle, and most importantly, a column on the right showing the Journal entry number. There is no column for amounts. The description column includes a complete description of the transaction. What, where, how, who, when, and how much. All Kipling's little servants.

This is a very simple Memorandum. Most firms may be computerized. Each individual set of documents must then be separately typed into the Memorandum, or a system set up so that the document is automatically entered into the Memorandum as soon as a document is raised. A system can be set up to type these documents in as soon as they are issued. This should minimize loss.

The Memorandum is the most vulnerable part of the accounting system. A system should be set up to make sure that ALL issued documents are entered into the Memorandum, all purchases and sales, all expenditure and receipts of any variety. This is a responsible task and should not be neglected. Persons doing this task should be high quality, conscientious and honest, and yes, highly paid. There should be at least two persons doing every task, and every missing item and non-correlating item should be double-checked.

The gap between issued documents and placing them on the accounting system is the Achilles heel of all accounting systems. Yes, systems can be set up to directly place computerized records of issued documents onto the Journal, as is often done nowadays, but there is no guarantee that the system will work. You need to separate recording the initial transaction and recording the transaction in the Journal, and there needs to be mutual checks, preferably by a common number.

Yes, many businesses find completing this Memorandum time consuming and feel that the time and effort spent doing it is wasteful, and many jump straight to the Journal, at least for regular transactions. But my opinion is that completing this Memorandum is an essential exercise. You may desperately need to track down some transaction, or what is worse, non-transaction, at any point in time.

My advice is that even if you have a myriad of transactions, thousands of invoices coming and going, records of cash transactions and so on, it is well worth going to the expense and trouble to record all purchases and sales, all paper documents issued in time order, before placing these transactions in the Journal. Brook no excuses to the contrary.

Furthermore, there should be a column on the right-hand side recording the Journal number. This cross-checks the transaction against the Journal. This record alone closes off a major source of fraud right at the start, non-entry, and massively improves the efficiency of your bookkeeping system (and maybe even massively increases your profits).

A properly operated Memorandum Book system is not a waste of resources. Having such system, made to operate rigorously, will save you a lot of money! For most firms, I am sure, it will create an amazing increase in profits.

CHAPTER 5

THE JOURNAL

Many accounting systems however start with the Journal.

There are many different specialist Journals used in modern accounting practice for convenience – Cash Receipts Journal, Cash Payments Journal, Sales Journal, Purchases Journal…… However, the description here will confine itself to the General Journal. All the above transactions can appear in the General Journal. If your business is large or expands you can obtain advice on what specialist journals you need.

An example below shows the appearance of the Journal without any entries:

JOURNAL (Example).

Date	Reference Number	Description	Debit	Credit

A General Journal or Journal normally contains five columns. The column on the left contains the date of the transaction. The next column contains the Reference Number, often called the Journal Number.

The next column contains the Description of the transaction. Now we start moving into double entry bookkeeping. It is a requirement of double entry bookkeeping that *two* entries are made in the books. This starts in the Journal. Each of these entries refers to a single Ledger account of the same name, and also if you are using a Memorandum, each of these entries refers back to a Memorandum entry.

Finally, there are two columns. The first is designated the Debit column. The second is designated the Credit column.

In this Journal you make two entries for each transaction. After entering the date and the Journal number, which is the consecutive number of every entry in the Journal, you first write the Account for which you are going to make the Debit entry. You write the Account Name in the Description column, and then in the Debit column the amount being Debited. Then on the next line write the name of the Account being Credited, and place the amount being Credited in the Credit column.

This is what happens for all Journal entries. A more detailed description of the methodology is described in the following chapters.

Pacioli advocated a slightly different system. Pacioli had a very concise Journal using the words *Per* and *A* divided by // on a single line. What he said was "…..there are two expressions used in the said Journal; one is called "*per*" and the other is called "*a*" each of which has a meaning of its own. "Per" indicates the debtor one or more as the case may b, and "a" a creditor, one or more as the case may be. At the beginning of each entry, we always provide "per", because, first, the debtor must be given, and immediately after the creditor, the one separated from the other by two little slanting parallels, thus, //, as the example below will show."

"Per cash// A – Capital of myself and so on. 56 Lire 76 Soldi, 24 Grossi, 16 Picoli."

Pacioli then says to draw a single diagonal line along the entry in the memorandum book after you have made the transfer into the Journal, to show that the item has been posted into the Journal.

In the course of time, the appearance of the Journal has been transformed in appearance into what I believe is a clearer entry, though taking up more space – separate lines for a Debit and Credit for the same transaction. I suppose paper in those days was more expensive! However, one thing has not changed. The bookkeeper must make a judgment at the stage of entering a transaction into the Journal, not the Ledger, on what is a Debit ("per") and what is a Credit ("a").

CHAPTER 6

BASIC ACCOUNTING THEORY

From here we can go off in several directions. But it is necessary to understand what Credit and Debit means, otherwise we cannot begin to place entries in the Journal.

Right, we will start with a bit of theory.

The following four-square boxes sometimes appear in textbooks.

THE FOUR-SQUARE METHODOLOGY

ACTIVITIES WHEN YOU INCREASE THE VALUE OF AN ACCOUNT

	DEBIT		CREDIT	
STOCKS	ASSETS	A	LIABILITIES	L
FLOWS	EXPENSES	E	INCOME	I

ACTIVITIES WHEN YOU DECREASE THE VALUE OF AN ACCOUNT

	CREDIT		DEBIT	
STOCKS	ASSETS	A	LIABILITIES	L
FLOWS	EXPENSES	E	INCOME	I

Now *Assets* are *what you own.*

Liabilities are *what you owe* to other people.

Income is money that you *receive*.

Expenses are money that you *pay*.

Income and Expenses are either actual current cash payments, or credit transactions (what you borrow from and lend to others). As you will see, double entry bookkeeping leaps over to credit transactions without taking a breath.

Now what are Debits and Credits? These terms stem from early Italian words, used by Pacioli, the Medicis, the Uffizis, and all those Medieval Italian Merchant.

Debit stems from the Latin *debere*, to owe.

Credit stems from the Latin *credere*, to believe.

So, accounts are divided into a four square, in a somewhat arbitrary division, with the terms and definitions going back to early medieval times. Yet it seems to make some sort of sense.

Remember first, these accounts refer to your business, not to you personally. What Pacioli wrote "..it is not wise to enter all your personal property and real property in this book. This book is kept on account of volume of business…", in other words you and your business are quite separate. So, if your business has Assets, it owes *you* the value of the Assets, Debit. Similarly, if the business has debts or liabilities, you or someone else *believes* that this money will be repaid to them, this amount is a Credit.

Similarly, though this is a bit harder to understand, if the business has expenses, it *owes* someone the value of the expenses, a Debit. If the business has income, you or someone else *believes* the money will be paid to the business, a Credit.

Thus, in double entry bookkeeping, you *Debit* an Expense and an Asset, and *Credit* an Income and a Liability to *increase* the value of that account.

Similarly, if you want to *decrease* the value of an account, you *Credit* an Expense and Asset, and *Debit* an Income and Liability.

That is the logic. **Your business is not you. It is a separate entity, and treats you and any other person the same.**

Even if you are a sole trader, and your business is not incorporated, you and the business are separate, and treated by the accounts as such. For example, suppose your name is John Smith, and you begin trading as a business. **You and the business are not the same for accounting purposes.** The business is different – "John Smith, Sole Trader", and though you may think the equity capital you used to set up the business is your own money, it is now in possession of your business - in this case "John Smith,

Sole Trader", and the **business owes you** the equity capital. That is why it is a **Liability** of the business. All the other Credits and Debits are ordered under that assumption – it is not you, it is your business that is trading.

So always keep this concept in mind, you and your business are separate, and are treated as such in the accounts.

I might add that many people find the above four-square diagrams difficult to memorize and can get confused. Most accountants and bookkeepers try to learn the methodology by rote, but from my experience most get confused and forget.

But what is helpful is an easy way to remember this requirement. A mnemonic. The following chapter describes such a mnemonic.

CHAPTER 7

DEAR CILLA

A long time ago, when I was learning accounting, the lecturer recited this mnemonic. He explained that Cilla Black (a famous entertainer at that time) was the patron saint of accounting. - "*Laughter*." He went on to say, "Cilla BLACK has RED hair, and as such she is the patron saint of all accountants", he said. - "*Groans*". "We shall use Dear Cilla's name to help you understand the bookkeeping process." - "*Screams*".

He then wrote on the board the words

DEAR CILLA

If you are bright and alert, you will immediately see some connections with bookkeeping.

DEA and CIL.

And what do they stand for?

D stands for Debit.
E stands for Expenses.
A stands for Assets.

Thus DEA stands for Debit Expenses and Assets.

C stands for Credit.
I stands for Income.
L stands for Liabilities.

CEA stands for Credit Expenses and Liabilities.

So, all you have to do is recite DEAr CILla, and you have a mnemonic. This is a mnemonic for all occasions if you want to INCREASE the value of that account.

So when you want to *increase* the value of an account, and the account is an *Expense* or *Asset,* you *Debit* that account. DEA. If the account is an *Income* or a *Liability* you *Credit* the value of the account. CIL.

In the Journal and Ledger, when you Debit, you write the value in the Debit column. Just write the value in that column. Don't add it up or anything.

In the Journal or Ledger, when you Credit, you write the value in the Credit column. Just write the value in that column. Don't add it up or anything.

The Converse. DECREASING the value of an account.

CEAR DILLA

Yes, as you will find, you will often also have to *decrease* values of an account.

How do you do that.

You Credit Expenses and Assets. CEA

You Debit Income and Liabilities. DIL

So, when you want to DECREASE the value of an account, just repeat to yourself,

CEAr DILla

Just keep the mnemonics DEAr CILla and CEAr DILla in your minds, and when we go onto the actual double entry process you won't be the least bit confused!

MEMORY PHRASE

There is a very simple phrase that all accountants can remember! Especially if you are a fan of the red-haired pop star Cilla Black! Dear Cilla!

DEAr CILla

Which means

DEBIT Expenses and Assets

CREDIT Income and Liabilities

When you are INCREASING the value of an account.

The converse, when you are DECREASING the value of an account, is

CEAr DILla

Not so memorable perhaps, but means

CREDIT Expenses and Assets

DEBIT Income and Liabilities

When you are DECREASING the value of an account.

NOTE. There is NO adding or subtracting!

Increasing and decreasing the account is conducted by placing the entry into either the debit or credit column of that account.

"Every debit has a credit, and every credit has a debit."

Chapter 8

PACIOLI'S JOURNAL

You have seen above a diagram of a blank General Journal. The time has come to fill it in.

You may remember Pacioli had a very concise Journal (after completing the Memorandum) using the words *Per* and *A* divided by // on a single line. This was very concise, but this methodology has fallen out of favor. After a close look at this methodology I have come to a reason for this fall from favor.

It would be automatically assumed by many tyro accountants that *Per* would correspond to a Debit and *A* would correspond to a Credit, and would be used as such in the Ledger!!! But this ain't necessarily so!!! Sometimes Per corresponds to a Credit and A corresponds to a Debit. Unless the clever bookkeeper moved the *Per* and *A* around in the Journal when necessary, this could lead to error in the Ledger. As you will see shortly, by using the mnemonic you can avoid this trap.

I'll give an example. Suppose Pacioli borrowed 1000 Ducats from his banker Snr Bertomolo, and placed that money in his till. He would increase his liability with Snr Bertomolo by 1000 Ducats and increase cash in the till by 1000 Ducats. But what would happen if Pacioli wrote "*Per* Snr Bertomolo //*A* cash 1000"? He would *Debit* the loan account with with Snr Bartomolo, and *Credit* Cash.

As you can see from DEAr CILla above, that is the wrong thing to do! To increase your loan account (a liability) you must *Credit* it, and to increase your Cash account you must *Debit* it. Early on, bookkeepers developed a clearer system for the Journal entries.

This method used today is as follows. I shall use the same transaction of borrowing 1000 Ducats from Snr Bertomolo and placing the money in the till.

JOURNAL (Example).

Date	Reference Number	Description	Debit	Credit
13 June 1500	512	Cash	1000	
13 June 1500	513	Snr Bertomolo		1000

As you can see, the entry into the Journal is now made in terms of Debits and Credits. The format is somewhat larger than Pacioli's system, having the Date, Journal number, the two account names in the description, plus the Debit and Credit amounts. Cash is *increased* by debiting it (as it is an asset A), DEAr, and the loan with snr Bertomolo is *increased* by crediting it, CILla, as it is a liability L. Just keep DEAr CILla and CEAr DILla going in your head!

It is an accounting convention that in the Journal the Debit entry is always made first, and appears above the Credit entry.

Thus, in the course of time since Pacioli's day, the double entry transaction has been brought forward to the Journal. That book is now all-important. The Ledger transaction has been reduced to a copy of the Journal entry, as you will see.

Using the Memorandum example in Chapter 4 above, I will proceed to give a few examples of Journal entries. Remember for each Memorandum entry, in the Journal **two** entries need be made, a Debit and a Credit.

However, before that you will need a list of Account names.

Chapter 9

Chart of Accounts

The reader might find it slightly irritating with all this dodging around, but to proceed to a knowledge of bookkeeping, a number of elements need to be known simultaneously. One of them is the location of the accounts, and an index of their names.

Right at the start, when setting up the accounting system, a list of account names needs to be made. This list carries the technical name "Chart of Accounts". In the old days of paper ledgers, this list was placed on the first page of the Ledger, with a page number against each item, referring to the page of the Account. Even in small firms the number of the accounts could number several hundred, and often they were not in alphabetical order, especially as accounts were added later in the course of time.

Nowadays with computerized accounting systems, the Chart of Accounts is on the very first page of the accounting system, and the most easily accessible. From there, by selecting the account name, it is usually easy to jump directly to the account required.

An example of a Chart of Accounts is given below. Sometimes for ease of explanation and use, the Chart of Accounts is divided into four sections; Assets, Liabilities, Revenue and Expenses. However, this is not technically necessary, and with modern computerized systems you most often get a straight list that you can even arrange in alphabetical order.

LEDGER PAGE 1
CHART OF ACCOUNTS

CHART OF ACCOUNTS		LEDGER PAGE
ASSETS	CASH ON HAND	1
	CASH AT BANK	2
	STOCK OF MANUALS	3
	BRENDON BLACK	15
	TIM WALSHAW	17
LIABILITIES	LOANS TO CLUB	4
	DISTRICT SUPPLIES	16
INCOME	MEMBERSHIP DUES	5
	BANK INTEREST	6
	CONTEST ENTRY	7
	RAFFLES	8
EXPENSES	DUES PAID TO INTERNATIONAL HQ	9
	TROPHY EXPENSES	10
	POST OFFICE BOX	11
	CONTEST EXPENSES	13
	BANK FEES	14

Note the four divisions: Assets, Liabilities, Income and Expenses.
They are important for what comes next.

As the Brendon Black, Tim Walshaw and District Supplies accounts were added later, their accounts are on later pages of the Ledger, and they have later page numbers! The layout of the Ledger can get pretty complicated and the Chart of Accounts page soon becomes an essential reference.

For those who are a bit more advanced in bookkeeping, you will notice that this set of accounts lacks an income account titled 'cost of supplies purchased', and an expenses account titled 'cost of goods sold'. There is a reason for this, and this will be explained fully in the chapter on "Inventories". At this stage, I will only say that this area is an accounting dilemma, an area that accounting teachers love to shoot through without stopping. This book will fully describe the issues, this logical paradox, and you can, indeed must, make an informed choice.

Chapter 10

And back again to the Journal

As we said, for every entry in the Memorandum, **two** entries need to be made in the Journal, a Debit and a Credit.

The decisions made here need to be of some moment. You need to make two important decisions simultaneously:

1. Chose two account names to match the transaction recorded in the Memorandum
2. Decide which account entry is the Debit and which is the Credit.

You must then make the entries in the Journal: Date, Journal Number, Account Names – the Debit first and the Credit second, and finally the same amount that appears in the Memorandum in the correct column, Debit or Credit.

No wonder bookkeepers sometimes got confused! In a later chapter, we shall see how this confusion is finally corrected.

Going back up to the Memorandum shown Chapter 4, we take the first entry from the Memorandum. This is the entry dated 25 July 12, Journal number 123.

Issued receipts no 541 to 551 to Ollie Ayrton, Sue Rabbidge, James Chatfield, Annie Ajmera, James Burson, Lutana McLeod, Brendon Black, Tim Walshaw, For Membership Dues $54 cash each.

So what happens here?

First look at the Chart of Accounts. You are dealing with an *Asset* account, Cash on Hand.

Also what else? An *Income* account. Membership Dues.

Note that Cash on Hand is *increased* and is an *Asset. Debit Assets* A to *increase* it. DEAr.

Membership Dues are *Income*. As more money coming in, the balance on the Membership Dues account is *increased*, *Credit Income* I to *increase* Income. CILla.

JOURNAL (Example).

Date	Reference Number	Description	Debit	Credit
25 July 12	123	Cash on Hand	540	
25 July 12	123	Membership Dues		540

Got that? There are four steps in the process. Go through these four steps every time.

1. First you look up the Chart of Accounts to identify the required accounts (two).
2. Ask yourself whether each account is an Asset or a Liability or Income or an Expense.
3. Identify whether you are i*ncreasing* or *decreasing* ***each*** account. (Note that you could be increasing or decreasing ***both*** accounts at the same time. The common presumption that if one side goes up the other must go down is not necessarily true. For example, if you increase cash revenue, cash on hand must also increase. It is basically common sense. Think about it. Don't try to go by rote). (This is a common trap in exams – be warned).
4. Use DEAr CILla for increasing the respective accounts, and CEAr DILla for decreasing the respective accounts.

In the case of the above example, you Debit Cash on Hand, DEAr, as you are increasing an Asset, and Credit Membership Dues, CILla, as you are increasing the total value of an Income account. (The latter might be a bit difficult to understand. But remember as you receive more income, the value of the Income account gets added to and cumulates).

As you go through these exercises you will discover that the double entry process is foolproof. There is a place for everything, and it all balances.

We move onto the next item in the Memorandum, dated 26 July 12, Journal number 124.

Deposited $540 at Bank. Bank receipt for $540. Westfield Bank receipt no 214870.

Note there are two entries implied here. You are reducing the value of the account Cash on Hand, and increasing the size of your bank balance, the value of the account Cash at Bank.

Reducing the size of your Cash on Hand is easy. Cash on Hand is an *Asset*. You *Credit* the account Cash on Hand. CEAr. You are reducing an asset.

But what is a Bank Balance? If you look the Chart of Accounts above you will see that it is called Cash at Bank. It is also an *Asset*. You are *increasing* an *Asset*. *Debit* Cash at Bank. DEAr.

JOURNAL (Example).

Date	Reference Number	Description	Debit	Credit
25 July 12	123	Cash on Hand	540	
25 July 12	123	Membership Dues		540
26 July 12	124	Cash at Bank	540	
26 July 12	124	Cash on Hand		540

Note that there are now two Journal transactions following one another. As the number of transactions increase, each transaction is added to the end of the previous one in the Journal.

Note here that sometimes DEAr and CEAr occur in the same transaction. Also CILla and DILla may occur in the same transaction. DEAr may not be followed by CILla and CEAr may not be followed by DILla. Don't automatically assume that it does! The correct technique is to check if the item is an Asset or Liability, and whether you are increasing or decreasing it.

We now go on to the next item in the Memorandum. Dated 27 July. Item number 125.

Purchased three trophies for speaking contest. $20 each. Paid check no 8476 99. $60. Carter Trophies receipt no 6174. $60

So what happened here? You are purchasing of trophies (see Chart of Accounts above). That is *Expenditure*. You are *increasing* the Trophy Expense account. *Increase* an *Expenditure* account? DEAr. *Debit.*

You paid by check. You are *reducing* the size of your bank account, Cash at Bank, an *Asset*. CEAr. *Credit.*

JOURNAL (Example).

Date	Reference Number	Description	Debit	Credit
25 July 12	123	Cash on Hand	540	
25 July 12	123	Membership Dues		540
26 July 12	124	Cash at Bank	540	
26 July 12	124	Cash on Hand		540
27 July 12	125	Trophy Expense	60	
27 July 12	125	Cash at Bank		60

Next item on the Memorandum. Getting a bit bored? Once you learn the technique it should come automatically.

Purchased refreshments for contest. Tim Walshaw Paid cash. $50. Hellas Club receipt no 5480. Check refund to Tim Walshaw for cash paid for refreshments. $50. Check no 847 00.

Now these appear to be two transactions. However, from the firm's (club's) point of view there was only one transaction. Tim Walshaw is not the Club. He is refunded $50 by Club check.

JOURNAL (Example).

Date	Reference Number	Description	Debit	Credit
25 July 12	123	Cash on Hand	540	
25 July 12	123	Membership Dues		540
26 July 12	124	Cash at Bank	540	
26 July 12	124	Cash on Hand		540
27 July 12	125	Trophy Expense	60	
27 July 12	125	Cash at Bank		60
30 July 12	126	Tim Walshaw	50	
30 July 12	126	Cash at Bank		50

So, what happens? The Club pays a check to Tim Walshaw, and Cash at Bank is reduced by $50.

Reduce an *Asset*, Cash at Bank. CEAr. *Credit*. Increase an *Asset*. Tim Walshaw's account. Debit. DEAr. See how it all works out?

Tim Walshaw is *Asset* account! Now this may worry some students. Why is Tim Walshaw a club asset? Remember technically, you have not actually *paid* Tim Walshaw, just transferred money to his account from the Bank account. In Double Entry Bookkeeping you are just moving figures around on the internal bookkeeping system.

But you wish to identify this payment as an expense – Contest Expense. This is where you recognize that money has flowed out of the Club. So, you do a reverse of this transaction, and *Credit* Tim Walshaw and *Debit* Contest Expense. Yes, it can be done. You are effectively *reducing an asset*, and *increasing* the total of an *expense* account. Think about it, it is perfectly logical. You are effectively moving a transaction around in the Balance Sheet! This is technically known as a *Contra* transaction.

JOURNAL (Example).

Date	Reference Number	Description	Debit	Credit
25 July 12	123	Cash on Hand	540	
25 July 12	123	Membership Dues		540
26 July 12	124	Cash at Bank	540	
26 July 12	124	Cash on Hand		540
27 July 12	125	Trophy Expense	60	
27 July 12	125	Cash at Bank		60
30 July 12	126	Tim Walshaw	50	
30 July 12	126	Cash at Bank		50
30 July 12	126	Contest Expense	50	
30 July 12	126	Tim Walshaw		50

OK, we are rolling. But let's get the next item in the Memorandum. Date 1 August. No 127.

Received Entrance fees for contest. $5 each. $150.

A very common entry. Cash sales. An accountant can do this blindfolded, but let's see what you can do.

Back to the Chart of Accounts. The item is obviously *increasing* Cash on Hand, an *Asset*. DEAr. A Debit.

What is the other account? If you go back to the Chart of Accounts it is Contest Entry, an *income account*. You are *increasing* the total value of an income account. CILla. A Credit.

JOURNAL (Example).

Date	Reference Number	Description	Debit	Credit
25 July 12	123	Cash on Hand	540	
25 July 12	123	Membership Dues		540
26 July 12	124	Cash at Bank	540	
26 July 12	124	Cash on Hand		540
27 July 12	125	Trophy Expense	60	
27 July 12	125	Cash at Bank		60
30 July 12	126	Tim Walshaw	50	
30 July 12	126	Cash at Bank		50
30 July 12	126	Contest Expenses	50	
30 July 12	126	Tim Walshaw		50
1 Aug 12	127	Cash on Hand	150	
1 Aug 12	127	Contest Entry		150

We now come to the next item in the Memorandum. Date 2 August. No 128.

Deposited $150 at Bank. Bank receipts $150. Westfield Bank receipt no 214871.

It is obvious what is happening here. Cash at Bank is increasing by $150, and Cash on Hand is decreasing by $150. Both are Assets.

Increase Cash at Bank. *Asset. Debit*. DEAr.
Decrease Cash on Hand. *Asset. Credit*. CEAr.

JOURNAL (Example).

25 July 12	123	Cash on Hand	540	
25 July 12	123	Membership Dues		540
26 July 12	124	Cash at Bank	540	
26 July 12	124	Cash on Hand		540
27 July 12	125	Trophy Expense	60	
27 July 12	125	Cash at Bank		60
30 July 12	126	Tim Walshaw	50	
30 July 12	126	Cash at Bank		50
30 July 12	126	Contest Expenses	50	
30 July 12	126	Tim Walshaw		50
1 Aug 12	127	Cash on Hand	150	
1 Aug 12	127	Contest Entry		150
2 Aug 12	128	Cash at Bank	150	
2 Aug 12	128	Cash on Hand		150

Now we go onto Credit transactions. Reason for panic? Reason for doing things different?

Chapter 11

Credit Transactions

The vast majority of transactions in today's commerce are credit transactions. Yet there is nothing mysterious about the bookkeeping process of credit transactions, as explained in the following very simple examples. And no, we do not need to resort to red ink and a different process.

We will now do a very simple credit transaction. This process is repeated on a large scale by most firms when they sell for credit. But aside from the sometime use of specialist credit accounts the bookkeeping process is fundamentally very simple. Text books, especially the older variety, try to bamboozle students with bank loans and bills of exchange. Their treatment is perfectly simple and logical, as you will see.

Suppose the Club purchases a stock of manuals on Credit, and 30 days later repays this amount by check. The Club buys 20 manuals at $4 each, total cost $80. It will later sell them at $5 each, a profit each of $1.

So - Debit the stock account, an Asset, DEA, as you are increasing it, and Credit the seller's account, a Liability, CIL, as you are increasing that also. No mention of loans or borrowing! Simple.

Below is the entry in the Memorandum.

Club purchase on 30 day credit from District Supplies 20 manual at $4 each. $80

What is happening here? First you are *increasing* the *Asset* account Stock of Manuals, DEAr. *Debit.*

The other account is District Supplies. It is a *Liability* account, which you are i*ncreasing*. CILla. *Credit.*

The Journal is as follows:

JOURNAL (Example).

Date	Reference Number	Description	Debit	Credit
25 July 12	123	Cash on Hand	540	
25 July 12	123	Membership Dues		540
26 July 12	124	Cash at Bank	540	
26 July 12	124	Cash on Hand		540
27 July 12	125	Trophy Expense	60	
27 July 12	125	Cash at Bank		60
30 July 12	126	Tim Walshaw	50	
30 July 12	126	Cash at Bank		50
30 July 12	126	Contest Expenses	50	
30 July 12	126	Tim Walshaw		50
1 Aug 12	127	Cash on Hand	150	
1 Aug 12	127	Contest Entry		150
2 Aug 12	128	Cash at Bank	150	
2 Aug 12	128	Cash on Hand		150
3 Aug 12	129	Stock of Manuals	80	
3 Aug 12	129	District Supplies		80

That is your first step in a credit transaction, Yes, it looks no different than all the other non-credit transactions. No red ink or special notation!

Now Brendon Black purchases a manual for $5. As he did not have money on him at the time, the manual was sold to him on credit.

The Memorandum entry appears as follows:-

Sold a Manual on Credit to member Brendon Black $5

So, Debit Brendon Black's account and Credit another, in this case the Asset account Stock Manuals. Both are Asset accounts.

Why Debit Brendon Black? You are *increasing* the value of one of the Club's *asset* accounts, called Brendon Black. DEAr. Brendon is now a *Debtor* to the Club, and owes it money. *Debit* the Brendon Black account.

The Club *reduces the value* of its stock of manuals by $5. That is another *asset* account. *Credit* an asset account to reduce it. CEAr. Credit Stock of Manuals. (No, we are not talking about profits here. Profits come out in the wash).

The Journal now looks like:

JOURNAL (Example).

Date	Reference Number	Description	Debit	Credit
25 July 12	123	Cash on Hand	540	
25 July 12	123	Membership Dues		540
26 July 12	124	Cash at Bank	540	
26 July 12	124	Cash on Hand		540
27 July 12	125	Trophy Expense	60	
27 July 12	125	Cash at Bank		60
27 July 12	126	Tim Walshaw	50	
27 July 12	126	Cash at Bank		50
27 July 12	126	Contest Expenses	50	
27 July 12	126	Tim Walshaw		50
1 Aug 12	127	Cash on Hand	150	
1 Aug 12	127	Contest Entry		150
2 Aug 12	128	Cash at Bank	150	
2 Aug 12	128	Cash on Hand		150
3 Aug 12	129	Stock of Manuals	80	
3 Aug 12	129	District Supplies		80
6 Aug 12	130	Brendon Black	5	
6 Aug 12	130	Stock of Manuals		5

Next, in a few days time, Brendon Black repays the Club $5 with cash. This appears in the Memorandum as follows:-

Brendon Black repays Club $5 for Manual

In this transaction, Brendon Black's account is *Credited*, as it's value is *reduced*, (yes, it now has zero balance) and the Cash on Hand account is Debited, for the $5, as it is *increased*. (Yes, in this case an account is reduced and another increased – but be warned, it does not happen every time!)

JOURNAL (Example).

Date	Reference Number	Description	Debit	Credit
25 July 12	123	Cash on Hand	540	
25 July 12	123	Membership Dues		540
26 July 12	124	Cash at Bank	540	
26 July 12	124	Cash on Hand		540
27 July 12	125	Trophy Expense	60	
27 July 12	125	Cash at Bank		60
27 July 12	126	Tim Walshaw	50	
27 July 12	126	Cash at Bank		50
27 July 12	126	Contest Expenses	50	
27 July 12	126	Tim Walshaw		50
1 Aug 12	127	Cash on Hand	150	
1 Aug 12	127	Contest Entry		150
2 Aug 12	128	Cash at Bank	150	
2 Aug 12	128	Cash on Hand		150
3 Aug 12	129	Stock of Manuals	80	
3 Aug 12	129	District Supplies		80
6 Aug 12	130	Brendon Black	5	
6 Aug 12	130	Stock of Manuals		5
12 Aug 12	131	Cash on Hand	5	
12 Aug 12	131	Brendon Black		5

Finally, the credit account at District Supplies for $80 is repaid, using a check drawn on the Bank.

The Memorandum entry is as follows:-

Account at District Supplies is paid by bank check $80

What does this mean? Cash at Bank, an *Asset* is *reduced* by $80. CEAr. A *Credit*. The account with District Supplies, a *Liability*, is *reduced* by $80. DILla. A *Debit*.

The Journal now looks like:

JOURNAL (Example).

Date	Reference Number	Description	Debit	Credit
25 July 12	123	Cash on Hand	540	
25 July 12	123	Membership Dues		540
26 July 12	124	Cash at Bank	540	
26 July 12	124	Cash on Hand		540
27 July 12	125	Trophy Expense	60	
27 July 12	125	Cash at Bank		60
27 July 12	126	Tim Walshaw	50	
27 July 12	126	Cash at Bank		50
27 July 12	126	Contest Expenses	50	
27 July 12	126	Tim Walshaw		50
1 Aug 12	127	Cash on Hand	150	
1 Aug 12	127	Contest Entry		150
2 Aug 12	128	Cash at Bank	150	
2 Aug 12	128	Cash on Hand		150
3 Aug 12	129	Stock of Manuals	80	
3 Aug 12	129	District Supplies		80

6 Aug 12	130	Brendon Black	5		
6 Aug 12	130	Stock of Manuals		5	
12 Aug 12	131	Cash on Hand	5		
12 Aug 12	131	Brendon Black		5	
14 Aug 12	132	District Supplies	80		
14 Aug 12	132	Cash at Bank		80	

As you can see, there are no problems with buying and selling on credit with Double Entry Bookkeeping. The whole process is handled smoothly without special procedures needed. No 'credit accounts', no separate accounting books and so on are required.

Now many students ask "Wow. Shouldn't credit accounts look different? Shouldn't they be separate? And colored red or something?"

The answer is that double entry bookkeeping smoothly handles "credit" transactions without even noticing it. They come out in the wash in the Balance Sheet when you get to it, but in the bookkeeping process you need not make any special provisions.

However, large firms often place their Debtors and Creditors accounts separately, so that they can be overseen and monitored, but that is not an essential part of the bookkeeping process.

Suppose the Club borrowed $1000 from the Bank. How is this treated? Let's say it starts a Bank Loan account. A *Liability* account, and it *increases* it by $1000. CILla

The money *increases* the Cash at Bank account, an *Asset.* DEAr

What happens here?

Debit the Cash at Bank account by $1000 and credit the Bank Loan account by $1000. Reverse the transaction when the loan is repaid.

JOURNAL (Example).

Date	Reference Number	Description	Debit	Credit
1 Sep 12	134	Cash at Bank	$1000	
1 Sep 12	134	Bank Loan		$1000

It is not intended in this book to cover more complex Journal entries, such as Depreciation, Appreciation, Credits, Discounts, Returns, Bills of Exchange and so on. Such items are dealt with in more detailed references, though the process is very simple. It is basically selecting the correct accounts, deciding whether you are going to increase or decrease their values, and crediting or debiting them. If your accounts have specialized requirements, I suggest that you take accounting advice on what accounts to set up. But essentially Double Entry Bookkeeping handles all accounting requirements.

So, there you are. You should by now be able to handle most Journal entries, for any firm, big or small.

The credit entries are very common. The firm buys goods on credit, often processes them, and sells goods from stock on credit. Such credit accounting transactions happen by the million every day, and are the backbone of the trading system, along with direct cash sales. Yet the accounting process is very simple. Nothing special happens. No special accounting is needed for credit purchases or sales. If separate credit accounts, even departments, are needed, they are there for the purpose of supervising the amount of credit taken and given, not making the entries.

So, you should now have no problem handling any Journal entry. Remember the four steps. 1. Refer to the Chart of Accounts. What are the two accounts being transacted? 2. Referring to each of these accounts in turn. Is that account an Asset, Liability, Income or Expense? 3. Are you increasing or decreasing the value of this account? 4. Remember DEAr CILla or CEAr DILla. Carry out the transaction and insert the correct Debit and Credit for each of the correct two accounts in the Journal. That's all!

Contra Transactions

Contra transactions have been previously mentioned briefly. Contra transactions occur where the accountant wants to make an adjustment to the accounts. There are two reasons for this type of transaction.

1. As its name implies, one purpose is to reverse the value of all or part of a transaction. Supposing for example, some goods you have sold have been returned, and you have agreed to refund the purchase price.
   When the goods were sold, the value of these goods had been credited to increase the value of a sales account, an income account, CILla; and the cash at hand account was debited, as its value increased. DEAr.
   Part of the value of the sales account is now reduced by the refund. The sales account is debited by the value of the refund, as it is reduced. DILla. Cash at hand is credited by the same amount as it is decreased. CEAr.
2. Another frequent use is to move amounts around in the accounts, usually to change the type of a transaction from a stock to a flow, or vice versa. For example, changing a decreasing value of an asset to expenses, or an increasing value of an asset to income.
   When you depreciate an asset, you decrease its value. You credit this asset account by the amount of the depreciation. CEAr. What do you do with the debit? You could debit decreasing income or liabilities, DILla, but it is more logical to debit expenses to increase expenses. DEAr. And that is what is done. Expenses are normally tax deductible. So, by a bookkeeping sleight of hand, depreciation is converted into a tax deduction.
   Similarly, increases in asset values can be converted into income! Suppose your assets increase in value, and you wish to show these increases in value on the books. To add to an asset value you debit that asset. DEAr. What can you credit? CILla or CEAr. Obviously when an asset value increases, you do not increase liabilities or decrease expenses. You increase income. CILla. So, accountants happily increase income by revaluing assets. Perfectly legally. In fact, they do it all the time. The fact that there may have been no increase in sales or business activity is irrelevant!

   Account analysts such as Warren Buffet hone in on contra transactions, and strip the accounts of these deceiving measures in order to obtain a more truthful view of a company's activities.

   Yes, there are accounting rules. The accounting bodies try to keep the use of Contra accounts to the bare minimum. If you work for a firm that appears to use Contra accounts excessively (do an Enron) alert the authorities or get out, or do both.

Chapter 12

THE LEDGER

All transactions flow from the Journal to the Ledger.

Back in the old days this was a giant book (which was difficult to run away with) completed by a clerk such a Bob Cratchit with a quill pen. (Actually bookkeepers in those days were well paid and under worked, and stories tell of bank clerks starting at ten and indolently working till 4. Times have changed.) Nevertheless, the name Ledger is still used for giant computerized databases that have nothing to do with double entry bookkeeping, except for outward appearance.

While the description in this book talks about paper ledgers, this is only to make the process clear. A computerized system can be directly based on this description of paper ledger pages, and it would work very well. The essential requirement would be that there needs to be separate permanent electronic account pages laid out logically as a paper account page – date, journal number, corresponding account name, and credit and debit columns. In the recent past electronic storage was valuable, and often accounting records were collapsed into a single data base. Nowadays, given the vast availability of cheap electronic storage, this is no longer necessary. I call for all computerized accounting systems to be urgently revised to directly reflect the appearance of the accounting system described in this book – that is all accounts should have a separate permanent page in the computer's electronic memory, as well as a separate Journal, and a separate Memorandum.

The appearance of a Ledger page is shown below:-

Example of a
Ledger page
ACCOUNT
NAME OF ACCOUNT

Date	Reference Number	Account	Debit	Credit
		"Debit the account" means insert the amount in the Debit column only. → Debit "Credit the account" means insert amount in the Credit column only. → Credit Note. There are no additions or subtractions in these accounting entries.		

Another type of ledger page is the "T" account, where the names of the other account and the amount are placed on the left or right side of a central divide. The left-hand side holds the debit entries, and the right-hand side the credit entries.

Some textbooks show a sixth column, which they call the "Balance", with an appearance rather like a Bank Statement. This layout is not to be recommended. To obtain a Balance you need a hidden cumulative total of both Debits and Credits, and then take one from the other. The computational requirements are major, even with an electronic system, and no useful function is served. In the next chapters, as you will see, such a Balance is obtained on a regular basis. Until then, keep it simple.

So, what is the process of the ledger entry? There is a formal method.

Back in the "old days", sixty or seventy years ago, when the bookkeeper, directly entering into the Ledger from the Day Book, really earned his money. He not only had to interpret what accounts the entry was made into, but whether it is a Debit or Credit.

Since then, as already been described, the Day Book dropped out, but entries were made directly into a modern Journal with Debits and Credits, and the names of both accounts are entered.

That has made things simpler for entering into the Ledger, but worse for auditing as there is nowadays no Memorandum! Oh well.

The essential point of the Ledger is that you now make entries onto **two separate pages**, called Accounts. You have to turn from one to another. You do not have it all on a single page, as in the Journal. (I am of course talking about a physical ledger. With computerized bookkeeping, the Ledger remains in name only in the computer memory. Separate pages can be called up, but the data is often maintained in a single database to save memory. The "page" you see on the screen is only a computerized reconstruction. In most computerized systems the Ledger does not continue to exist in practice as separate pages.)

How do you start?

You start with the most recent entries in the Journal.

All those entries that have already been entered into the Ledger are crossed out, or to use the old-fashioned term "struck out". It is essential that as soon as you complete a Ledger entry you "strike out" the relevant Journal entry. Pacioli recommended a different system, placing marks against the relevant entries in the Journal. Over time as usage evolved, the "strike out" was found to be more effective.

Indeed, when you make a Journal entry, also it is necessary to strike out the relevant entry in the Memorandum. Alternatively, and this is preferable, you enter the Journal Number against the Memorandum entry. That way you will quickly see what entries have not been entered in the Journal, and eventually in the Ledger. Nevertheless, a mere strike out or number entry is no evidence of entry into the following book. Pacioli advises a regular audit between all the books. As he advises "for this you need two persons, and everything is carefully checked against one another".

As has already been said, the Journal has the following information: the date of entry, the Journal number, the names of two Accounts, and an amount entered as a Debit or Credit against each account.

From this entry, two entries are made into *separate* pages on the Ledger, a Debit and a Credit. Both these entries are copied from the Journal entry, which has hopefully been correctly completed.

An example is shown in the following boxes, copying from the completed Journal above. The first Journal entry is:

Date	Reference Number	Description	Debit	Credit
25 July 12	123	Cash on Hand	540	
25 July 12	123	Membership Dues		540

As can be seen here, it is necessary to select two Account pages in the Ledger, Cash on Hand and Membership Dues.

How do we find them? Turn to the "Chart of Accounts" page in the Ledger, look up the account names, find the page number, and turn to that page number.

Which page do you turn to first? Out of ancient custom, you turn to the Debit entry page first. This is in this case, *Cash on Hand.*

A Ledger page has five columns: the Date column on the left, then the Journal Number column, then the Account column, then the Debit column, and then the Credit column.

You need to make a Debit entry on the Ledger page for Cash on Hand of $540.

You first insert the Date of the entry in the left-hand column.

You then insert the Journal Number in the next column, obtained from the Journal.

Now we come to the Account column. Remember we are dealing with **two** accounts here, Cash on Hand and Membership Dues, as we are doing double entry.

Which Account page are we on? Cash on Hand.

Which Account name shall we place in this account column? *Membership Dues.*

Shall we Debit or Credit the amount - $540? The Journal says *Debit* Cash on Hand.

Place $540 in the Debit column. *NOTE that this Debit refers to the account name at the head of that page. In this case Debit the Cash on Hand account.*

You will note that that a *different* name has been placed in the Account column. In this case *Membership Dues. But you are NOT debiting Membership Dues, but the Cash on Hand account.* This is a common mistake of confused students. Don't get confused!

This is shown in the following box.

LEDGER ACCOUNT
CASH ON HAND

Date	Reference Number	Account	Debit	Credit
25 July 12	123	Membership Dues	$540	

This is your first Ledger entry. But it is not completed yet. You need to make a double entry onto another Account page.

Turn to the Membership Dues Account. Now what account do you place in the Account column? Cash on Hand.

Insert the Date and Journal number in their respective columns.

Now, do we Debit or Credit the $540. According to the Journal, Credit.

You have credited Membership Dues.

This is shown in the following box.

LEDGER ACCOUNT
MEMBERSHIP DUES

Date	Reference Number	Account	Debit	Credit
25 July 12	123	Cash on Hand		$540

So, you have Debited the Cash on Hand account, and Credited the Membership Dues account. You have placed the name Membership Dues in the Account column of the Cash on Hand Account while placing the name Cash on Hand in the Account column of the Membership Dues account. Don't forget to complete the Date and Reference Number columns.

You have completed your first double entry in the Ledger! Pat yourself on the back!

The next thing to do is "strike through" the completed Journal entry.

JOURNAL (Example).

Date	Reference Number	Description	Debit	Credit
25 July 12	123	Cash on Hand	540	
25 July 12	123	Membership Dues		540

You have now completed your first double entry in total!

"Strike throughs" have been used for a least a couple of centuries with good results. If you are doing the accounts by hand it is not "old fashioned" to do this. If you are using a computer (assuming you have a Journal), make sure that the computer does the equivalent.

Do you want to do a few more Ledger entries? We shall continue through the Journal above.

Note that for the purpose of simplification, it is assumed that all the Ledger Debit and Credit balances start at zero on these accounts. More on this later.

NEXT transaction. Look at the next Journal entry.

Date	Reference Number	Description	Debit	Credit
25 July 12	123	Cash on Hand	540	
25 July 12	123	Membership Dues		540
26 July 12	124	Cash at Bank	540	
26 July 12	124	Cash on Hand		540

You have two Accounts here, Cash at Bank and Cash on Hand. (Note that the previous Journal entry has been "struck out".)

Which is the Debit? Cash at Bank. $540 is Debited to the Cash at Bank account. Cash on Hand is the opposing Credit account.

So, turn to the Cash at Bank account. Insert the date and Journal number.
What do you do here? The opposing Credit entry is for Cash on Hand. Insert the name Cash on Hand in the Account column.

Then insert $540 in the Debit column.

LEDGER ACCOUNT
CASH AT BANK

Date	Reference Number	Account	Debit	Credit
26 July 12	124	Cash on Hand	$540	

Now we turn to the Credit entry. Which account is it? Cash on Hand.

Enter the date and Journal number. The write the name of the opposing account, Cash at Bank, in the Account column.

What is it? A Credit or a Debit? A Credit. How much? $540. Write $540 in the credit column.

LEDGER ACCOUNT
CASH ON HAND

Date	Reference Number	Account	Debit	Credit
25 July 12	123	Membership Dues	$540	
26 July 12	124	Cash at Bank		$540

Above is the Cash on Hand account entry. You place Cash at Bank under the account name and Credit $540.

As you can see there is already a previous entry in the Cash on Hand account, Debiting $540 for the account Membership Dues.

So, you have copied the above Journal entry and placed in the account Cash at Bank a credit entry for $540.

So, what has happened here? $540 was received as Membership Dues. It was debited to Cash on Hand, and then transferred to Cash at Bank, a credit. This is your second Ledger entry!

Remember the previous Journal entry is struck out. From now on, we speed things up. If you get confused go back to the beginning of the chapter.

We strike out this Journal entry.

Date	Reference Number	Account	Debit	Credit
~~25 July 12~~	~~123~~	~~Cash on Hand~~	~~540~~	
25 July 12	123	Membership Dues		~~540~~
~~26 July 12~~	~~124~~	~~Cash at Bank~~	~~540~~	
26 July 12	124	Cash on Hand		~~540~~

What is the next Journal entry?

The Club bought trophies with a check for $60. What two accounts are you going to use? Trophy Expense. Debit. Cash at Bank. Credit.

JOURNAL (Example)

Date	Reference Number	Description	Debit	Credit
~~25 July 12~~	~~123~~	~~Cash on Hand~~	~~540~~	
25 July 12	123	Membership Dues		540
~~26 July 12~~	~~124~~	~~Cash at Bank~~	~~540~~	
26 July 12	124	Cash on Hand		~~540~~
27 July 12	125	Trophy Expense	60	
27 July 12	125	Cash at Bank		60

The following are the Ledger entries.

First the Debit entry. In this case Trophy Expense for $60.

The Trophy Expense account page is selected. Cash at Bank is written into the account column. $60 is written into the Debit column.

LEDGER ACCOUNT
TROPHY EXPENSE

Date	Reference Number	Account	Debit	Credit
27 July 12	125	Cash at Bank	$60	

The Cash at Bank page is then selected. The account name Trophy Expense is placed in the Account column, and $60 is placed next to it in the Credit column.

Note that the Cash at Bank account has now two entries, Cash on Hand and Trophy Expense.

LEDGER ACCOUNT
CASH AT BANK

Date	Reference Number	Account	Debit	Credit
26 July 12	124	Cash on Hand	$540	
27 July 12	125	Trophy Expense		$60

Next Journal entry. The Club holds a contest. Tim Walshaw, a club member initially pays the $50 cost. He is refunded by the Club.

JOURNAL (Example).

Date	Reference Number	Description	Debit	Credit
25 July 12	123	Cash on Hand	540	
25 July 12	123	Membership Dues		540
26 July 12	124	Cash at Bank	540	
26 July 12	124	Cash on Hand		540
27 July 12	125	Trophy Expense	60	
27 July 12	125	Cash at Bank		60
30 July 12	126	Tim Walshaw	50	
30 July 12	126	Cash at Bank		50

What happens here? Tim Walshaw's account is Debited $50 and Cash at Bank is Credited $50.

LEDGER ACCOUNT
TIM WALSHAW

Date	Reference Number	Account	Debit	Credit
30 July 12	126	Cash at Bank	$50	

LEDGER ACCOUNT
CASH AT BANK

Date	Reference Number	Account	Debit	Credit
26 July 12	124	Cash on Hand	$540	
27 July 12	125	Trophy Expense		$60
30 July	126	Tim Walshaw		$50

Then that respective Journal entry for $50 is ruled out. The next transaction is the Contra entry previously mentioned, where payment to Tim Walshaw is transferred to Contest Expenses for accounting purposes. The Club needs to keep a tag on Contest Expenses.

JOURNAL (Example).

Date	Reference Number	Description	Debit	Credit
25 July 12	123	Cash on Hand	540	
25 July 12	123	Membership Dues		540
26 July 12	124	Cash at Bank	540	
26 July 12	124	Cash on Hand		540
27 July 12	125	Trophy Expense	60	
27 July 12	125	Cash at Bank		60
28 July 12	126	Tim Walshaw	50	
28 July 12	126	Cash at Bank		50
30 July 12	126	Contest Expenses	50	
30 July 12	126	Tim Walshaw		50

The first ledger account is a Debit, Contest Expenses.

LEDGER ACCOUNT
CONTEST EXPENSES

Date	Reference Number	Account	Debit	Credit
30 July 12	126	Tim Walshaw	$50	

The next account is a Credit. Tim Walshaw.

LEDGER ACCOUNT
TIM WALSHAW

Date	Reference Number	Account	Debit	Credit
30 July 12	126	Cash at Bank	$50	
30 July 12	126	Contest Expenses		$50

Now you can see the basic reason for Double Entry. The entries for each of the accounts are separated, and they can be seen as part of a separate entity. Also now this information in in a form that can be manipulated further into useful formats that provide further useful information.

The next item is cash paid for entry into a contest, $150. The Journal entry is as follows:

JOURNAL (Example).

Date	Reference Number	Description	Debit	Credit
25 July 12	123	Cash on Hand	540	
25 July 12	123	Membership Dues		540
26 July 12	124	Cash at Bank	540	
26 July 12	124	Cash on Hand		540
27 July 12	125	Trophy Expense	60	
27 July 12	125	Cash at Bank		60
30 July 12	126	Tim Walshaw	50	
30 July 12	126	Cash at Bank		50
30 July 12	126	Contest Expenses	50	
30 July 12	126	Tim Walshaw		50
1 Aug 12	127	Cash on Hand	150	

1 Aug 12	127	Contest Entry		150	

The Debit account is Cash on Hand. Contest Entry goes into the Account column.

LEDGER ACCOUNT
CASH ON HAND

Date	Reference Number	Account	Debit	Credit
25 July 12	123	Membership Dues	$540	
26 July 12	124	Cash at Bank		$540
1 Aug 12	127	Contest Entry	$150	

The Credit account is the Contest Entry account. Cash on Hand goes into the Account column.

LEDGER ACCOUNT
CONTEST ENTRY

Date	Reference Number	Account	Debit	Credit
30 July 12	126	Cash on Hand		$150

The respective Journal entry for $150 is then ruled out.

Note that the entries in the Cash on Hand account is growing.

Next Journal entry. The $150 is deposited in the Bank.

There are two accounts here, Cash at Bank, Debit, and Cash on Hand, Credit.

JOURNAL (Example).

Date	Reference Number	Description	Debit	Credit
25 July 12	123	Cash	540	
25 July 12	123	Membership Dues		540
26 July 12	124	Cash at Bank	540	
26 July 12	124	Cash		540
27 July 12	125	Trophy Expense	60	
27 July 12	125	Cash at Bank		60
30 July 12	126	Tim Walshaw	50	
30 July 12	126	Cash at Bank		50
30 July 12	126	Contest Expenses	50	
30 July 12	126	Tim Walshaw		50
1 Aug 12	127	Cash on Hand	150	
1 Aug 12	127	Contest Entry		150
2 Aug 12	128	Cash at Bank	150	
2 Aug 12	128	Cash on Hand		150

LEDGER ACCOUNT
CASH AT BANK

Date	Reference Number	Account	Debit	Credit
26 July 12	124	Cash on Hand	$540	
27 July 12	125	Trophy Expense		$60
30 July 12	126	Contest Expense		$50
2 Aug 12	128	Cash on Hand	$150	

LEDGER ACCOUNT
CASH ON HAND

Date	Reference Number	Account	Debit	Credit
25 July 12	123	Membership Dues	$540	
26 July 12	124	Cash at Bank		$540
1 Aug 12	127	Contest Entry	$150	
2 Aug 12	128	Cash at Bank		$150

And of course, the last Journal entry is then ruled out.

Buying and selling on credit

We now move on to buying and selling on credit. This is probably the most common activity, after selling for cash, that businesses transact. Yet the process is perfectly simple.

Taking the next Journal entry. In this transaction the Club purchases on credit a set of 20 manuals from District Supplies, the supplier for $80. The Journal is shown below.

JOURNAL (Example).

Date	Reference Number	Description	Debit	Credit
25 July 12	123	Cash on Hand	540	
25 July 12	123	Membership Dues		540
26 July 12	124	Cash at Bank	540	
26 July 12	124	Cash on Hand		540
27 July 12	125	Trophy Expense	60	
27 July 12	125	Cash at Bank		60
30 July 12	126	Tim Walshaw	50	
30 July 12	126	Cash at Bank		50

30 July 12	126	Contest Expenses	50	
30 July 12	126	Tim Walshaw		50
1 Aug 12	127	Cash on Hand	150	
1 Aug 12	127	Contest Entry		150
2 Aug 12	128	Cash at Bank	150	
2 Aug 12	128	Cash on Hand		150
3 Aug 12	129	Stock of Manuals	80	
3 Aug 12	129	District Supplies		80

So, Debit the Account Stock of Manuals, as you are increasing it, an Asset, DEAr, and Credit the account of District Supplies, as you are increasing a Liability, CILla That's all. *No special credit account needs to be set up.*

LEDGER ACCOUNT
STOCK OF MANUALS

Date	Reference Number	Account	Debit	Credit
3 Aug 12	129	District Supplies	$80	

LEDGER ACCOUNT
DISTRICT SUPPLIES

Date	Reference Number	Account	Debit	Credit
3 Aug 12	129	Stock of Manuals		$80

Next Brendon Black buys a manual for $5. As he had no cash on him at the time, the club sold him the manual on Credit. The Journal says:

JOURNAL (Example).

Date	Reference Number	Description	Debit	Credit
25 July 12	123	Cash on Hand	540	
25 July 12	123	Membership Dues		540
26 July 12	124	Cash at Bank	540	
26 July 12	124	Cash on Hand		540
27 July 12	125	Trophy Expense	60	
27 July 12	125	Cash at Bank		60
27 July 12	126	Tim Walshaw	50	
27 July 12	126	Cash at Bank		50
27 July 12	126	Contest Expenses	50	
27 July 12	126	Tim Walshaw		50
1 Aug 12	127	Cash on Hand	150	
1 Aug 12	127	Contest Entry		150
2 Aug 12	128	Cash at Bank	150	
2 Aug 12	128	Cash on Hand		150
3 Aug 12	129	Stock of Manuals	80	
3 Aug 12	129	District Supplies		80
6 Aug 12	130	Brendon Black	5	
6 Aug 12	130	Stock of Manuals		5

Brendon Black is Debited $5, as his account is an Asset and increasing. DEA. Club Stock of Equipment and Manuals is Credited $5 as the account is an asset and is decreasing. CIL.

The Ledger transactions are as follows:

LEDGER ACCOUNT
BRENDON BLACK

Date	Reference Number	Account	Debit	Credit
10 Aug 12	130	Stock of Manuals	$5	

LEDGER ACCOUNT
STOCK OF MANUALS

Date	Reference Number	Account	Debit	Credit
10 Aug 12	130	Brendon Black		$5

Next Brendon Black repays the $5 using cash. This is shown in the Journal entry:

JOURNAL (Example).

Date	Reference Number	Description	Debit	Credit
25 July 12	123	Cash on Hand	540	
25 July 12	123	Membership Dues		540
26 July 12	124	Cash at Bank	540	
26 July 12	124	Cash on Hand		540
27 July 12	125	Trophy Expense	60	
27 July 12	125	Cash at Bank		60

	30 July 12	126	Tim Walshaw	50		
	30 July 12	126	Cash at Bank		50	
	30 July 12	126	Contest Expenses	50		
	30 July 12	126	Tim Walshaw		50	
	1 Aug 12	127	Cash on Hand	150		
	1 Aug 12	127	Contest Entry		150	
	2 Aug 12	128	Cash at Bank	150		
	2 Aug 12	128	Cash on Hand		150	
	3 Aug 12	129	Stock of Manuals	80		
	3 Aug 12	129	District Supplies		80	
	6 Aug 12	130	Brendon Black	5		
	6 Aug 12	130	Stock of Manuals		5	
	12 Aug 12	131	Cash on Hand	5		
	12 Aug 12	131	Brendon Black		5	

As you can see above, the account Cash on hand is Debited, as it is an asset an increasing, DEA, and the account of Brendon Black is Credited as it is an Asset and decreasing. CIL.

LEDGER ACCOUNT
CASH ON HAND

Date	Reference Number	Account	Debit	Credit
25 July 12	123	Membership Dues	$540	
26 July 12	124	Cash at Bank		$540
1 Aug 12	127	Contest Entry	$150	
2 Aug 12	128	Cash at Bank		$150
24 Aug 12	131	Brendon Black	$5	

LEDGER ACCOUNT
BRENDON BLACK

Date	Reference Number	Account	Debit	Credit
10 Aug 12	130	Club Stock of Equipment and Manuals	$5	
24 Aug 12	131	Cash on Hand		$5

The debt to District Supplies has to be paid off by a check drawn on the bank for $80 nearly a month later.

The Journal shows as follows

JOURNAL (Example).

Date	Reference Number	Description	Debit	Credit
25 July 12	123	Cash on Hand	540	
25 July 12	123	Membership Dues		540
26 July 12	124	Cash at Bank	540	
26 July 12	124	Cash on Hand		540
27 July 12	125	Trophy Expense	60	
27 July 12	125	Cash at Bank		60
30 July 12	126	Tim Walshaw	50	
30 July 12	126	Cash at Bank		50
30 July 12	126	Contest Expenses	50	
30 July 12	126	Tim Walshaw		50
1 Aug 12	127	Cash on Hand	150	
1 Aug 12	127	Contest Entry		150
2 Aug 12	128	Cash at Bank	150	
2 Aug 12	128	Cash on Hand		150
3 Aug 12	129	Stock of Manuals	80	
3 Aug 12	129	District Supplies		80
6 Aug 12	130	Brendon Black	5	
6 Aug 12	130	Stock of Manuals		5
12 Aug 12	131	Cash on Hand	5	
12 Aug 12	131	Brendon Black		5
14 Aug 12	132	District Supplies	80	
14 Aug 12	132	Cash at Bank		80

The account District Supplies is Debited $80, as it is a Liability and it is being decreased, DIL, and Cash at Bank is also being decreased by $80, but it is an Asset, Credit, CEA.

Note that both these accounts are being decreased at the same time. Not one increased and the other decreased, as many bookkeeping tyros often assume!
The Ledger entries are as follows:

LEDGER ACCOUNT
DISTRICT SUPPLIES

Date	Reference Number	Account	Debit	Credit
3 Aug 12	129	Club Stock of Equipment and Manuals		$80
30 Aug 12	132	Cash at Bank	$80	

LEDGER ACCOUNT
CASH AT BANK

Date	Reference Number	Name	Debit	Credit
26 July 12	124	Cash on Hand	$540	
27 July 12	125	Trophy Expense		$60
30 July 12	126	Tim Walshaw		$50
2 Aug 12	128	Cash on Hand	$150	
30 Aug 12	132	District Supplies		$80

So, the above is an example of a credit transaction. Goods are bought on credit, and eventually the supplier is paid. Simple!

You may be saying that most credit transactions are a lot more complicated than this. No they are not! ALL credit transactions take the same form, whether buying $80 of supplies, or buying a $100 million tanker for Shell. The transaction appears in the books basically as the above.

Finally, the last transaction in the Journal has to be struck out, as follows:

JOURNAL (Example).

Date	Reference Number	Description	Debit	Credit
25 July 12	123	Cash on Hand	540	
25 July 12	123	Membership Dues		540
26 July 12	124	Cash at Bank	540	
26 July 12	124	Cash on Hand		540
27 July 12	125	Trophy Expense	60	
27 July 12	125	Cash at Bank		60
27 July 12	126	Tim Walshaw	50	
27 July 12	126	Cash at Bank		50
27 July 12	126	Contest Expenses	50	
27 July 12	126	Tim Walshaw		50
1 Aug 12	127	Cash on Hand	150	
1 Aug 12	127	Contest Entry		150
2 Aug 12	128	Cash at Bank	150	
2 Aug 12	128	Cash on Hand		150
3 Aug 12	129	Stock of Manuals	80	
3 Aug 12	129	District Supplies		80
6 Aug 12	130	Brendon Black	5	
6 Aug 12	130	Stock of Manuals		5
12 Aug 12	131	Cash on Hand	5	
12 Aug 12	131	Brendon Black		5

	14 Aug 12	132	District Supplies	80		
	14 Aug 12	132	Cash at Bank		80	

So there you are! You now know how to do Double Entry Bookkeeping! The theory is simple, but the operation can be confusing.

To summarize the process briefly:

1. First, you enter the details of all transactions, big or small, in the Memorandum book.
2. You enter in turn the values of each transaction from the Memorandum into the Journal, as both Debits and Credits, naming two correctly selected accounts chosen from the Chart of Accounts in the Journal entry. Use DEAr CILla and CEAr DILla as mnemonics to guide your choice of Debits and Credits.
3. From the Journal, enter the transaction into two separate Ledger accounts, one as a Debit and the other as a Credit.

There. Simple! If you follow the correct procedure every time you should have no trouble.

Chapter 13

The Credit Accounts

Yes, I said that Double Entry Bookkeeping deals with credit seamlessly. Nonetheless, all firms, aside from the smallest, separate out the "Credit Accounts" and supervise them separately.

What are Credit Accounts? They are accounts where the outstanding Debits and Credits are not cleared immediately, but wait for a period before they are cleared. There are standard and customary lengths for these periods, "thirty days", "sixty days", "ninety days" and even "one hundred and twenty days".

Now these accounts are also customarily divided into two groups, "Debtors" and "Creditors". Accounts Receivable and Accounts Payable. For the holders of the Debtor accounts, they owe you money. For the holders of the Creditor accounts, you owe them money.

Debtor accounts are accounts where there is a net Debit balance.

Creditor accounts are accounts where there is a net Credit balance.

Take a "thirty day" debt on a Creditor account. These are normally your suppliers from whom you have obtained an agreement to pay 30 days after the receipt of their invoice. An "Invoice" is essentially a bill requesting payment for goods or services delivered. It customarily has a line printed on it saying something like "Payment due in thirty days from receipt of goods delivered" or "...from receipt of invoice". All this is customary law, a custom that has grown up over centuries, and has a legal basis in the "Law of Merchant" in most advanced economies.

Towards the end of thirty days in the case of thirty-day credit, you are required to send the seller a check for the amount on this invoice, in legal terms "acquit the terms of the invoice".

Similarly, for a Debtor account, you send out an invoice to the buyers of your goods and services on the date you provided the goods or services, stating in how many days you expect the stated payment for these goods and services.

So, all businesses, with hardly any exception, offer and receive credit for the goods and services they buy and sell, and expect to pay or receive payment at the end of the stated period. The exceptions are retailers, who receive cash for their goods. Some businesses pay cash to their suppliers, usually because they have a bad or unknown credit rating.

As I said, in Double Entry Bookkeeping, no special provisions are made for credit transactions. But in practice, firms set Debtor and Creditor accounts aside for special supervision. The reason is that in Double Entry Bookkeeping there is no automatic alert to say when accounts should be paid. You need a human supervisor to oversee these accounts to make sure the accounts are paid on time.

Often this credit control activity is split up into two separate areas, the Debtors department and the Creditors department, that supervise the timely payment and receipt of these accounts. *It must be stressed however, even though these departments oversee these accounts, the actual bookkeeping is carried out separately by the bookkeeping or accounting departmen*t.

So that is the Credit supervision process. However, as you might surmise, the actual receipt and payment of accounts on time when they are due is a fraught area tied up with a lot of very human decision making.

As you will see at the end of this book, timeliness of payments is tied up with a very important, even vital, consideration, **cash flow**. The crucial measure of Cash Flow is the **coincident** receipt and payment of money. If you receive payments late, your cash flow is reduced. If you pay late, your cash flow is enhanced. So, in the business world, there is constant tension between firms on how fast they customarily, as apart from what they are required to, pay their accounts.

My advice to any businessperson is; - only deal with firms that customarily pay on time (if you can); and similarly, always pay your own accounts on time.

In practice only dealing with prompt payers is difficult. How do you find initially who are prompt payers, unless from bitter experience? I suggest that an excellent source of information on this subject is the firm of Dun and Bradstreet, who provide credit reports on all firms trading everywhere. A Dun and Bradstreet credit report provides an assessment on how fast a particular firm pays its accounts. A fast payer gets a good credit rating. Your firm will also be on a Dun and Bradstreet report, so I strongly advise pay promptly.

What happens if customer pays late, but is too important for you to stop supplying to it (the customer has a high proportion of your sales)? I suggest that first you increase your prices on them, if you can, to cover the cost and risk. At the same time, I suggest that you sell the debt to people called "Factors" who buy such debts, specifying a "no-recourse payment", and the Factor being responsible for chasing any late payment. If your customer won't go along with that arrangement, my strong advice is stop selling to them regardless, and take Court action for outstanding debts. **Cash flow** is crucial, and is a matter of survival. The number of firms that have gone under suddenly, caused by cash flow problems, caused in turn by a slow-paying major client, are legion. Don't be tempted. Don't stay with them. A controlled fall in profits is of secondary importance to the sudden drying up of cash flow. The risk of a slow paying major client destroying your company is too great. Do a scenario test – what will happen to your business if this slow payer suddenly extends payment time for another 30 days, or even stops paying?

You may say "Easier said than done". But at least I have alerted you to the necessity to extract yourself from selling to those slow paying firms. Squeeze up the price until they stop buying from you. Reducing sales gradually, under your control, is better than a sudden debacle, as these sorts of late-paying firms have no scruple in stopping buying from you overnight. I have seen it done.

Chapter 14

Bank Reconciliation

Before we go on to Trial Balance we need to discuss Bank Reconciliation, as an un-reconciled ledger can lead to trouble. If the cash balances to not reconcile it is a sure sign of either inefficiency or theft, or both. This process needs to be done first always.

For those who have heard of the process of Bank Reconciliation, the reaction is divided. There are those who say "Ho hum, it is just a matter of un-presented checks", and those who say "Horrors, I don't want to go near the subject!"

Well, it is a lot more complicated than just un-presented checks, but if taken step by step, it is easily handled.

So, what is Bank Reconciliation? Basically and ideally the *adjusted* balance on your Cash at Bank account has to exactly match at that point of time the balance in your account at the Bank. Note that the single account you have to look at is your CASH AT BANK account, not Cash on Hand, or any other. This makes it simpler at the start. Ideally this account should be a mirror image of the Bank Statement at that date; but yes, you have guessed it, it virtually never is.

There are those (a few) who never conduct this Bank Reconciliation exercise. Not doing this is an open invitation to those in your firm, who currently steal from you through un-accounted invoices or expense vouchers, to steal your cash as well!

You MUST regularly check the veracity of your Bank account. Some do it weekly. It is strongly advised that you do it at least monthly. The trigger MUST be at least when you receive your regular Bank Statement.

So, you have your latest Bank Statement. What do you do next?

There four items or headings under which there are differences between the Bank Statement and the Cash at Bank account.

1. Unpresented checks.
2. Unrecorded deposits.
3. Bank charges and interest.
4. Bank transfers.

Unpresented checks.

Suppose towards the end of the period you are looking at, you sent a check to another person or business. This amount the amount was recorded in your Cash at Bank as what? A reduction in your bank account value. CEAr. A Credit. Anyway, the amount appears in your Cash at Bank account.

However, the post takes several days, the other business' accounting process is slow, and the inter-bank clearing process is slow. By the time the check is cleared – that is Debited to your bank account, it could be a week or more. Your Cash at Bank account and the Bank Statement do not match up.

Unrecorded Deposits

This is rather unusual, but it happens. Suppose you had a bunch of cash and checks that you were going to deposit at the Bank that day. You recorded the amount as a Debit in the Cash at Bank account, but the Bank was closed when your employee reached the Bank, so he followed instructions by placing the bag in the safe deposit box. The amount was not credited to your account until next day, but the Statement was closed the previous day. There is no Credit on your bank statement for this amount.

Bank Charges and Interest

Both the items are Debited and Credited to your account without the Bank notifying you. The amounts may be small, but as a consequence the accounts do not balance.

Bank Transfers

Heretofore all textbooks up to a certain vintage talk about checks and cash. But times change. Electronic payments! They can be big. They can be unauthorized. These must be caught immediately. That is why, as previously said, I feel that that Bank Reconcilations should take place weekly, not monthly as in the olden times of check transfers.

Ah yes. Many a sad, sad story of a desperate accountant. Needing to borrow a big chunk of money. Will pay it back before the end of the month. But it was not to be. In this modern age, while there is always a requirement for two signatures on checks, how many firms have got across restricting the authorization requirements for electronic transfers? I still find two thirds of (small) firms I have dealt with use a single authorization for electronic transfers for unlimited amounts!

Anyway, electronic transfers **may** not appear in your Cash at Bank account even though they appear on the Bank Statement. If this happens, run, scream, cry, immediately to the most senior person you can get. Yes, there may be a good reason for the transfer. But if the boss does not know about it, he will head down the drain-pipe like a greased small mammal, have no fear about that. There will be a hue and cry until there is an explanation. And then you can complete your reconciliation.

The Bank Reconciliation Process

The bank reconciliation process consists of the following steps:

Step 1. Obtain *paper* copies of both the Cash at Bank account, and the Bank Statement. This job cannot be done "on-screen". In this day of computerized bookkeeping this needs to be a stated requirement.

Step 2. Rule in the start and finish dates in both the Cash at Bank account and the Bank Statement. Lay these paper copies side by side. Pick up a pencil.

Step 3. Compare the *Debit* column in the Cash at Bank account with the *Credit* column of the Bank Statement. Tick those items in both accounts where there is an agreement. (Remember you are not dealing in totals but individual amounts). Note that the dates need not coincide, but if the order of the transactions do not coincide, this should be a matter for investigation.

Step 4. Then compare the *Credit* column in the Cash at Bank account with the *Debit* column in the Bank Statement. Tick those items in both accounts where there is an agreement.

Step 5. Circle those items in both accounts that are *not* ticked.

Step 6. There are a number of circled items in the Bank Statement that need to be posted in the Cash at Bank account. Note, there should be an explanation for all these items. These items could be in the Bank Statement:

- Bank charges, a Debit.
- An electronic Bank transfer, a Debit. (Remember my warning above. *Immediately* check why this has not appeared in the accounts, and who authorized it). You will need a copy of a written authorization without delay for accounting purposes.
- Fees for check books and other services. Debit.
- Deposits. Credit. In this electronic transfer age, the incidence of money being transferred to your firm's account without you knowing about is increasing. It can be a real pain. You need the name of the account of the depositor, and hopefully a written explanation.
- Interest. Credit.
- Dividends by electronic transfer. Credit.
- Dishonored checks. A Debit. Unless the Bank alerts you, this one can slip through until the Bank Reconciliation.

Step7. I could go through an exercise of back-posting the above to the Cash at Bank account, but you know how to do it, don't you? Take the first example - Bank Charges. Credit Cash at Bank, and Debit the Bank Charges account. Second, credit Cash at Bank and Debit the account of the recipient (assuming the payment is authorized). Third, Credit Cash at Bank and Debit Check Book Fees. And so on....Remember post two accounts always.

For the last one, dishonored checks, the treatment can vary between firms. Credit Cash at Bank, Debit the customer's account. Then maybe Debit Bad Debts and Credit the customer's account.

Electronic transfers have now become a real pain in the Bank reconciliation process. Accountants and administrators have not fully got across this "Oh so convenient" form of money transfer. All I can recommend is heightened alertness by the bookkeeper, and insisting on obtaining written authorizations.

Step 8. Items in the Cash at Bank account that do not appear in the Bank Statement.

- Checks drawn and sent out, but have not been cleared. A Credit.
- Deposits into the firm's bank account that have not appeared on the Bank Statement. Debit. Pick up the phone to the Bank to check if the amount appears in the Bank account next day. If it does not, and if you cannot find an immediate explanation, wooooop! Straight upstairs!

Step 9. You now have an updated Cash at Bank account. But of course you cannot update the Bank Statement. You have outstanding (circled) Debits and Credits on this account.

Step 10. *Total* the Debit and Credit columns on the Cash at Bank account. Total the Debits and Credit columns on the Bank Statement. Onto the total of the Debit column on the Bank Statement, add the outstanding (circled) Credit items on the Cash at Bank account. Onto the total of the Credit column on the Bank Statement, and the outstanding (circled) items on the debit column on the Cash at Bank account.

Step 9. Both the totals of the Debit and Credit columns of the Cash at Bank account and the amended Debit and credit columns of the Bank statement should match.

Step 10. If they do not, subtract the totals of the Debit and Credit columns of both accounts from each other. Check through all the entries to see if there is a comparative amount missing; that you have made an arithmetical mistake; you have shifted a Debit to a Credit (and vice versa); or transposed a number. Given the limited number of transactions in most periods, the difference should not be hard to track down.

The following is an example of a Bank Reconciliation. It is for some other month than the examples above. There are two items to look at. The Bank Statement for July, and that part of the Cash at Bank Ledger account. They should exactly match, Debit for Credit, and Credit for Debit, but of course they do not…

Take printed copies of the Bank Statement and the Cash at Bank Ledger account for the same period and lay them side-by-side. Tick those transactions that match, Debit in one and Credit in the other, and vice versa. Then carefully search through both copies, and circle those items that do not match.

EASTGO BANK

Statement: Eastern Traders July 2012

Date	Particulars	Debit $	Credit $	Balance $
1 July	Balance			1050.00 Cr
3	Deposit		550.00✓	1600.00 Cr
6	Deposit		800.00✓	2400.00 Cr
8	Check 14976	640.00✓		1760.00 Cr
8	Deposit		425.00✓	2185.00 Cr
10	Bank Charges	(20.00)		2165.00 Cr
19	Check 14977	800.00✓		1365.00 Cr
20	Dividends (BP)		(200.00)	1565.00 Cr
21	Check book	(10.00)		1555.00 Cr
22	Check 14978	650.00✓		905.00 Cr
23	Dishon. Check – B. Toms	(105.00)		800.00 Cr
25	Interest		(10.00)	810.00 Cr
27	Bank transfer	(1100.00)		290.00 Dr
29	T. Noff – Direct Deposit		(250.00)	40.00 Dr

LEDGER ACCOUNT
CASH AT BANK

Date	Reference Number	Name	Debit	Credit
3 July	150	Cash on hand	550.00✓	
6 July	151	Cash on hand	800.00✓	
6 July	152	Powell Supplies		640.00✓
8 July	153	Cash on Hand	425.00✓	
16 July	155	Mumford Parts		800.00✓
19 July	157	Powell Supplies		650.00✓
30 July	160	Cash on Hand	(250.00)	
30 July	161	Mumford Parts		(350.00)

Now add to the Bank Statement and Cash at Bank Ledger account the missing items in both the Debit and Credit columns. You will see in the following examples that these items have been added in italic notation.

EASTGO BANK

Statement: Eastern Traders July 2012

Date	Particulars	Debit $	Credit $	Balance $
1 July	Balance			1050.00 Cr
3	Deposit		550.00	1600.00 Cr
6	Deposit		800.00	2400.00 Cr
8	Check 14976	640.00		1760.00 Cr
8	Deposit		425.00	2185.00 Cr
10	Bank Charges	20.00		2165.00 Cr
19	Check 14977	800.00		1365.00 Cr
20	Dividends (BP)		200.00	1565.00 Cr
21	Check book	10.00		1555.00 Cr
22	Check 14978	650.00		905.00 Cr
23	Dishon. Check – B. Toms	105.00		800.00 Cr
25	Interest		10.00	810.00 Cr
27	Bank transfer	1100.00		290.00 Dr
29	*T. Noff – Direct Deposit*		*250.00*	40.00 Dr
	Mumford Parts	*350.00*		
	Column totals	*3675.00*	*2235.00*	

You will note that a transfer of $1100 has been found that does not appear in the Cash at Bank Ledger account. If one of these appear unaccounted and unexplained transactions appear in the Bank Statement, and they often do, believe me, don't delay, but take the matter up immediately with senior management.

LEDGER ACCOUNT
CASH AT BANK

Date	Reference Number	Name	Debit	Credit
3 July	150	Cash on hand	550.00	
6 July	151	Cash on hand	800.00	
6 July	152	Powell Supplies		640.00
8 July	153	Cash on Hand	425.00	
16 July	155	Mumford Parts		800.00
19 July	157	Powell Supplies		650.00
30 July	160	Cash on Hand	250.00	
30 July	161	Mumford Parts		350.00
30 July	*162*	*Bank Charges*		*20.00*
30 July	163	*Check book*		*10.00*
30 July	164	*B. Toms*		*105.00*
30 July	165	*Dividends received*	*200.00*	
30 July	166	*Interest received*	*10.00*	
30 July	167	*B. Nipes*		*1100*.00
30 July		*Column totals*	*2235.00*	*3675.00*

This $1100 was transferred to B. Nipes, but no written authorization was passed to accounts. It happens!

So the column totals of $3675.00 and $2235.00 were reconciled between the Cash at Bank account and the Bank Statement. .

As I said, if taken step by step, Bank Reconciliation is a relatively easy process. But it MUST be carried out frequently. Indeed, it is advisable that you carry one out before you do a Trial Balance.

What happens to the items in italics in the Bank Statement is then a matter of firm policy. Some items are 'back posted'. Others are held over until the transactions flow through as normal. But what is essential – you are aware whether or not the Bank Statement is reconciled.

Finally, some firms present to management shortened bank reconciliation forms. There is no standard, so I won't go into those formats.

Chapter 15

Bringing Down the Balances

To produce a Trial Balance two things need to be done. The first is to produce a Net Balance for each account.

The second is transfer these balance of Debits and Credits to a list. This list is called a Trial Balance. If carried out correctly the sum of all the Debits should equal the sum of all the Credits.

Yes, your computer can do this, maybe, without your help. But can you do it without the computer? Can you tell if the computer is correct? This description tells you how to obtain a trial balance if the computer has crashed, and all you have are print-outs of the account pages.

How to obtain the balances for each account in the Ledger

There are simple steps taken one at a time.

1. First "Rule off" each account on the Balance Day, the day chosen for producing the Trial Balance. A horizontal line is drawn across the Ledger page of all the accounts on that day. In the old days this line was often drawn to with red ink, but any color may be used. Such accounts are then called "Ruled Off".

2. After the account is ruled off, the Debit and Credit columns are totaled. You will find that in the vast majority of cases the total of the Debits and Credits do not match. In many Ledger accounts there is blank or zero on one side or the other.

3. Dying to write the totals under the red line? Nope, don't do that yet. Draw a couple more lines (in black) a couple of spaces below the red line, on each side, to take the totals.

4. Write down the largest total first on the side that has the largest total, between these two lines.

5. Write the same total between the two lines on the other side.

6. It doesn't add up on that side? Yes, it does, if you add the difference between that total and the smaller total on that side. This is called the "Balance".

7. Add the name "Balance" in the description column. **Also** after Balance write the letters "c/d", which stands for "carried down". This is important, as you will see, and not some archaic accounting practice.

8. Now on the other side, a couple of spaces below the double lines, write "Balance b/d" and the figure. b/d stands for "brought down". The figure for the Balance b/d shifts from the Balance c/d column – shifting from the Credit to Debit column or the Debit to credit column.

9. Eventually you will have a list of values of balance b/d's and whether they are Debits or Credits. That is what you are aiming for.

10. Make a list of account names and balance b/d's for every account, Debits and Credits. This is your Trial Balance.

Yes, with a computer, you should be able to prepare a Trial Balance in a few seconds at a press of a button. In fact, here is a warning. If the computer starts chugging away and taking a lot of time, it is a good indication that you do not have a Double Entry accounting system. Everything is held in database single-entry form and has to be re-sorted to produce a Trial Balance. That is not a satisfactory state of affairs. Indeed, as many people who have computerized bookkeeping systems have learnt to their cost, it is a dangerous state of affairs. Single entry bookkeeping systems, using a single-entry database, are easily open to fraud, despite loud claims to the contrary.

Practical demonstration of completing a trial balance

I will list all the Ledger Accounts we have completed, together with their balance c/d's and balance b/d's.

A word of advice at the start. It is the usual practice to arrange the Trial Balance contents into two sections, the "stocks" and the "flows". The stocks, what become the Assets and the Liabilities, come first. Then the "flows", what become the income and expenses, come second. This is because it makes it easier to later divide the Trial Balance into a preliminary Balance Sheet and Profit and Loss Statement.

First "rule off". Many accounting textbooks nowadays do not show a rule off, but 100 years ago they all insisted on it. My personal opinion is that it is valuable to do it, as it shows definitely the date you are balancing.

Next rule two lines a short distance below the "rule off" line. As below.

LEDGER ACCOUNT
CASH ON HAND

Date	Reference Number	Account	Debit	Credit
25 July 12	123	Membership Dues	$540	
26 July 12	124	Cash at Bank		$540
1 Aug 12	127	Contest Entry	$150	
2 Aug 12	128	Cash at Bank		$150
10 Aug 12	131	Brendon Black	$5	

Next, total both columns and write in the total in the column with the largest total.

LEDGER ACCOUNT
CASH ON HAND

Date	Reference Number	Account	Debit	Credit
25 July 12	123	Membership Dues	$540	
26 July 12	124	Cash at Bank		$540
1 Aug 12	127	Contest Entry	$150	
2 Aug 12	128	Cash at Bank		$150
24 Aug 12	131	Brendon Black	$5	
			$695	

Yes, the two columns do not balance.

Now enter the balancing figure under the column with the lower figure. In this case add $5 to the credit column under the red line. Underneath Brendon Black write "Balance c/d" which means "Balance carried down".

The terms "carried down" and "brought down" are accounting terms whose origin is lost in the mists of time. The terms are vaguely meaningful. Don't worry, just use them.

LEDGER ACCOUNT
CASH ON HAND

Date	Reference Number	Account	Debit	Credit
25 July 12	123	Membership Dues	$540	
26 July 12	124	Cash at Bank		$540
1 Aug 12	127	Contest Entry	$150	
2 Aug 12	128	Cash at Bank		$150
24 Aug 12	131	Brendon Black	$5	
		Balance c/d		$5
			$695	$695

Next in the other column to the "Balance c/d" you write the same value, in this case $5. This is the "Balance b/d" figure.

LEDGER ACCOUNT
CASH ON HAND

Date	Reference Number	Account	Debit	Credit
25 July 12	123	Membership Dues	$540	
26 July 12	124	Cash at Bank		$540
1 Aug 12	127	Contest Entry	$150	
2 Aug 12	128	Cash at Bank		$150
24 Aug 12	131	Brendon Black	$5	
		Balance c/d		$5
			$695	$695
		Balance b/d	$5	

Why go to all this trouble? As you will see all these Balance b/d figures go to make the Trial Balance. A Trial Balance is a list of all the Balance b/d figures in the Debit and Credit columns.

And if you ask, why go to these peculiar lengths? The answer is simple. It works! After 500 years of practical use, it has been shown that this method always works! Not even your doctor can claim that.

So, we proceed with all the accounts to construct a Trial Balance.

The next item would be Cash at Bank

LEDGER ACCOUNT
CASH AT BANK

Date	Reference Number	Name	Debit	Credit
26 July 12	124	Cash on Hand	$540	
27 July 12	125	Trophy Expense		$60
30 July 12	126	Tim Walshaw		$50
2 Aug 12	128	Cash on Hand	$150	
30 Aug 12	132	District Supplies		$80
		Balance c/d		$500
			$690	$690
		Balance b/d	$500	

The next item would be Stock of Manuals.

LEDGER ACCOUNT
STOCK OF MANUALS

Date	Reference Number	Name	Debit	Credit
3 Aug 12	129	District Supplies	$80	
10 Aug 12	130	Brendon Black		$5
		Balance c/d		$75
			$80	$80
		Balance b/d	$75	

The next account is an Asset account, Brendon Black. It was quickly repaid. However as there were transactions in this account it needs to be ruled off.

LEDGER ACCOUNT
BRENDON BLACK

Date	Reference Number	Name	Debit	Credit
10 Aug 12	130	Club Stock of Equipment and Manuals	$5	
24 Aug 12	131	Cash on Hand		$5
		Balance c/d		0
			$5	$5
		Balance b/d	0	

It is necessary to account for zero balances in bookkeeping, and in Trial Balances.

Going down the Chart of Accounts, the next account is Tim Walshaw. Same process.

LEDGER ACCOUNT
TIM WALSHAW

Date	Reference Number	Name	Debit	Credit
28 July 12	126	Cash at Bank	$50	
28 July 12	126	Contest Expenses		$50
		Balance c/d		$0
			$50	$50
		Balance b/d	0	

We now move on to Liabilities accounts. These are Loans to the Club, and the account created later, District Supplies. However, Loans to the Club remained nil, and but strictly must appear in the Trial Balance. Even though District Supplies was paid off, it is ruled off and appears in the Trial Balance as zero. (You may question some of these standard requirements, but they were built up over time for good reasons).

LEDGER ACCOUNT
DISTRICT SUPPLIES

Date	Reference Number	Name	Debit	Credit
3 Aug 12	129	Club Stock of Equipment and Manuals		$80
30 Aug 12	132	Cash at Bank	$80	
		Balance c/d	0	
			$80	$80
		Balance b/d		0

Even though there is a nil balance on the District Supplies account at the end of the period, and b/d are shown as nil, this account must appear in the Trial Balance with a nil balance.

We next turn to the Income accounts in the Chart of Accounts. The first is Membership Dues.

LEDGER ACCOUNT
MEMBERSHIP DUES

Date	Reference Number	Name	Debit	Credit
25 July 12	123	Cash on Hand		$540
		Balance c/d	$540	
			$540	$540
		Balance b/d		$540

The Club received nil Bank Interest during this period. Again, this account is ruled off none the less, and appears as a nil Balance b/d. In which column? This is a good exercise.

LEDGER ACCOUNT
BANK INTEREST

Date	Reference Number	Name	Debit	Credit
30 July 12		Cash at Bank	$0	
		Balance c/d		$0
			$0	$0
		Balance b/d	$0	

If Bank interest had been received, this would have been an asset. This account would have been debited and Cash at Bank credited. So at least $0 is placed in that account in the Debit column before it is ruled off. So, the same procedure is followed as if $5 is placed in the debit column, and thus a Balance b/d of $0 is placed in the Debit column! Not that it makes any difference, you say. But it is best in accounting to be clear, neat and tidy. And not cut corners.

The next account in the Income section is Contest Entry.

LEDGER ACCOUNT
CONTEST ENTRY

Date	Reference Number	Name	Debit	Credit
30 July 12	126	Cash on Hand		$150
		Balance c/d	$150	
			$150	$150
		Balance b/d		$150

The next account in the Income section is Raffles. Alas, for the last contest, the Club did not sell any raffle tickets! If it had, it would have also purchased raffle prizes that would have appeared in Contest Expenses and also the payment would have appeared in Cash at Bank. So, the Raffles Account will appear in the Trial Balance with a zero balance. Where? In the Debit Column, of course. (if you are unsure, go to the above example and work it out).

The next accounts are in the Expenses section, starting with the account Dues Paid to International HQ. Things are getting a bit slack with this Club. If you check the Memorandum, you will find no dues have been paid to International HQ! If dues had been paid, the account Dues Paid to International HQ would have been Debited and the Cash at Bank account would have been Credited.

What is the column for the $0 balance in the Trial Balance? The Debit column.

The next account is Trophy Expenses. There has definitely been some expenses for this.

LEDGER ACCOUNT
TROPHY EXPENSE

Date	Reference Number	Name	Debit	Credit
26 July 12	123	Cash at Bank	$60	
		Balance c/d		$60
			$60	$60
		Balance b/d	$60	

The next expense is Contest Expense.

LEDGER ACCOUNT
CONTEST EXPENSES

Date	Reference Number	Name	Debit	Credit
30 July 12	126	Cash at Bank	$50	
		Balance c/d		$50
			$50	$50
		Balance b/d	$50	

That should be the lot. However, at this point check that you have not missed out an account. A common enough error. Take a copy of the Chart of Accounts and tick off *every* account against both the accounts you have closed off, and those with zero balances if you have not closed them off. (Strictly speaking, you close off *all* accounts, even those with zero balances, and carry out the balance c/d, balance b/d procedure with the zero balances).

To reduce this exposition to manageable proportions, it was assumed that in this period no dues were paid to International HQ, there were zero Bank Fees (ok this is not very realistic), and the Post Office Box fee is paid in the next period. Zero balances! Also the club did not raise any money using Raffles (slack!) and there were zero Loans to the Club.

Yet all these zero balances should appear in the Trial Balance.

We now proceed to do a Trial Balance.

Chapter 16

The Trial Balance

What is a Trial Balance? It is the sum of all the Debit and Credit totals of all the accounts in the Ledger. If these sums are equal, the Ledger is 'Balanced'.

As has been said, if you have a set of 'balance b/d's' this procedure should be very simple. (Indeed all double entry bookkeeping is very simple, *if* you rigorously follow the required procedures.)

So make a list of all the Debit b/d's and Credit b/d's.

You use three columns, the name of the account (using the Chart of Accounts), a Debit column, and a Credit column.

TRIAL BALANCE

NAME OF ACCOUNT	DEBIT BALANCES B/D	CREDIT BALANCES B/D
Cash on Hand	155	
Cash at Bank	500	
Club Stock of Equipment and Manuals	75	
Brendon Black	0	
Tim Walshaw		0
Loans to Club		0
Membership Dues		540
Bank Interest	0	
Contest Entry		150
Raffles	0	
Dues paid to International HQ		0
Trophy Expenses	60	
Post Office Box		0
Supplies Purchased from District Supplies		0
Contest Expenses	50	
Bank Fees	0	
TOTAL	*740*	*690*

Yes, it does not balance!

Most textbooks present a balanced Trial Balance as a fait accompli. Then present a list of things that *could* go wrong. The truth of the matter is that, unless you have one of those wonderful computerized systems, the Trial Balance will *always* go wrong. The painful part is finding what has gone wrong.

At this point, to relieve the tension I will tell a joke. The Bank of England's clerks always balanced the books at the end of the day. One evening the books would not balance. They were out by one penny! No clerk could go home until they found the error. There could be millions missing! They worked all night but just could not find the error. Dawn broke. A clerk was glancing down the books when he noticed one of the one's looked funny. He looked closely and brushed it. It was a fly's leg!

Here is a list of things to look for if the Trial Balance does not balance:

1. Errors of Omission. When a transaction is completely omitted from the accounting records. This is THE biggie. It's amazing how often it happens. It

also can lead to discovery of accounting fraud. Find it. Find out what happened. Look at it carefully.

2. Compensating Errors. Errors that cancel each other out on the Credit and Debit side. If it has not been deliberate, the chance that this has occurred is statistically small. However, you are dealing with thousands of figures, and honest errors of this type *do* occur.
3. Errors of Commission. When the entries are made at the correct amount, both debit and credit, but one or more entries are posted to the wrong account. If this happens, don't get mad at the bookkeeper. This was an honest error. If it keeps happening, retraining is required. It is hard to find honest and willing bookkeepers.
4. Errors of Reversal. When entries are made to the correct amount, but the debits are posted to credits, and vice versa. As above, don't get mad. It happens. A pained remark at the most, and if it happens again, retraining.
5. Error of Original Entry. When both the transaction amounts are wrong. This is up in the Errors of Omission category. How did it happen? What exactly went wrong? Yes, who was to blame? Make absolutely sure it does not happen again.

So back to this error in the Trial Balance example. The difference in the Credit and Debit balance is $740 - $690 = $50 debit.

So what does one do here?

First. Check the additions. Simple. But by this time you are tired, and can do the sums wrong, The Credits are OK.

Then check the entries into the Trial Balance from the balances b/d.

What's this? The very first one, Cash on Hand, should be $5, not $155!

So, do the Trial Balance again, this time with the correct figure.

TRIAL BALANCE

NAME OF ACCOUNT	DEBIT BALANCES B/D	CREDIT BALANCES B/D
	$	$
Cash on Hand	5	
Cash at Bank	500	
Club Stock of Equipment and Manuals	75	
Brendon Black	0	
Loans to Club		0
Membership Dues		540
Bank Interest	0	
Contest Entry		150
Raffles	0	
Dues paid to International HQ		0
Trophy Expenses	60	
Post Office Box		0
Supplies Purchased from District Supplies		0
Contest Expenses	50	
Bank Fees	0	
TOTAL	*690*	*690*

It works! The Trial Balance balances, $690 each side.

This means the accounting process has been conducted correctly. However, as the above list shows, things may not still be kosher. However, if the procedures have been followed correctly, as described in this book, from completing the initial Memorandum, through the Journal, and correctly placing two entries, a Debit and Credit in the Ledger, you would have a very high degree of confidence in the results.

From here the accountant takes over in order to derive a Balance Sheet and Profit and Loss Statement. However as will be shown in the next chapter, a very simple and useful and basic Balance Sheet and Profit and Loss statement can be derived immediately from the Trial Balance.

Chapter 17

A More Complex Trial Balance

While it would be possible to derive these statements from the above Trial Balance, it is a bit too short to supply a meaningful result. So, a slightly extended Trial Balance is used as an example. This Trial Balance reflects the accounts of a small manufacturing business.

TRIAL BALANCE
FRED'S MANUFACTURING LTD
As at 30 June 2012

NAME OF ACCOUNT	DEBIT BALANCES B/D	CREDIT BALANCES B/D
	$	$
Cash on Hand	200	
Stock at hand/inventory	30,000	
Plant and machinery	100,000	
Bank Loan overdraft/cash at bank		20,000
Buildings	570,000	
Accounts receivable	20,000	
Accounts payable		10,000
Shares nominal value		100,000
Accumulated capital		524,300
Sales Revenue		420,000
Discounts received		750
Rent Expense	750	
Raw material purchases	150,000	
Machinery purchases	50,000	
Wages and salaries	150,000	
Rates	1000	
Repairs	500	
Insurance	300	
Bank interest and charges	150	
Income Tax	400	
Postage	100	
Travel expenses	600	

Printing and stationary	400	
Discounts allowed	650	
TOTAL	*1,075,050*	*1,075,050*

No, these figures are not derived from a real-life enterprise. They are purely illustrative, and the relative values have been guessed.

If you are not sure why figures are placed on one side or another, - why Sales are a Credit and Accounts Receivable is a Debit, I suggest that you go back and trace the source of these figures step by step until the rationale thoroughly permeates you. Rest assured the whole process is thoroughly logical.

At this point, for most bookkeepers, you have come to the end of the game! Congratulations! The Accountant will take over from here, and often you will not recognize the final result. However, there is a short step you can take to achieve a 'nominal' Profit and Loss Statement and Balance Sheet. While these are not recognized as the final result under accounting rules (that is what Accountants are for), they nevertheless provide, in my opinion as an economist, a very real picture of where the enterprise is. Often these profits and balance sheets are more informative than the final ones provided by the accountant.

Chapter 18

Deriving a Balance Sheet and Profit and Loss Statement from a Trial Balance, and also deriving Cash Flow

At the very least a Trial Balance and the following dissection should be carried out on a monthly basis by any reasonably sized enterprise. If the Trial Balance shows that you made a short-term 'cash flow' loss, alarm bells should be ringing. (I have seen many small and also reasonably large firms get a rush of blood to their heads and go on a spending spree, or alternatively, sales suddenly fall over a cliff while the owners still have their heads in the clouds).

So how does one obtain a Profit and Loss Statement and Balance sheet from a Trial Balance?

We will look at the above Trial Balance below, but his time the 'stock' items are identified by being in italics.

TRIAL BALANCE
FRED'S MANUFACTURING LTD
As at 30 June 2012

NAME OF ACCOUNT	DEBIT BALANCES B/D	CREDIT BALANCES B/D
	$	$
Cash on Hand	*200*	
Stock at hand/inventory	*30,000*	
Plant and machinery	*100,000*	
Bank Loan overdraft/cash at bank		*20,000*
Buildings	*570,000*	
Accounts receivable	*20,000*	
Accounts payable		*10,000*
Shares nominal value		*100,000*
Accumulated capital		*524,300*
Sales Revenue		420,000
Discounts received		750
Rent Expense	750	
Raw material purchases	150,000	
Machinery purchases	50,000	
Wages and salaries	150,000	
Rates	1000	
Repairs	500	
Insurance	300	
Bank interest and charges	150	
Income Tax	400	
Postage	100	
Travel expenses	600	
Printing and stationary	400	
Discounts allowed	650	
TOTAL	1,075,050	1,075,050

We need to deal with the Income Statement/Profit and Loss Statement first, because the estimated net income is transferred as a Capital Item to the Capital Section (Liabilities) of the Balance Sheet. Any net profit the firm accumulates is added to capital at the end of the period.

Dissect the 'flow' items into Revenue and Expenses, and insert Totals for each of Revenue and Expenses. Divide the Expenses into Current Expenses and Capital Expenses, and insert sub-Totals. Insert a balancing item for net revenue. This could be a nominal Profit (positive) or a nominal Loss (negative).

TRIAL BALANCE
FRED'S MANUFACTURING LTD
As at 30 June 2012

Revenue and Expenses

Account Name	DEBIT BALANCES B/D	CREDIT BALANCES B/D
	$	$
Revenue		
Sales		420,000
Discounts receive		750
Total revenue		*420,750*
Expenses		
Current expenses		
Rent expense	750	
Raw material purchases	150,000	
Wages and salaries	150,000	
Rates	1000	
Repairs	500	
Insurance	300	
Bank interest and charges	150	
Income Tax	400	
Postage	100	
Travel expenses	600	
Printing and stationary	400	
Discounts allowed	650	
Total current expenses	*304,350*	
Capital expenses		
Machinery purchases	50,000	
Total capital expenses	*50,000*	
Total expenses	*354,850*	
Net revenue		*65,900*

If you get a negative net revenue, which is negative cash flow, this can be very serious indeed. This must be corrected immediately. If you are not already technically insolvent, and thus trading illegally, you *must* take immediate steps to increase sales or cut expenses until net revenue becomes positive.

Balance Sheet

Assets		*Liabilities*	
	$		$
Stock at hand 30 June 2012	30,000	Accounts payable	10,000
Cash on hand	200	Cash at Bank	20,000
Accounts receivable	20,000		
Buildings	570,000	*Total liabilities*	*30,000*
Plant and machinery	100,000		
		Equity	
		Share capital	100,000
		Accumulated capital at 30 June 2012	524,300
		Net revenue in period to 30 June 2012	65,900
		Total equity	*690,200*
Total Assets	*720,200*	*Total Liabilities and Equity*	*720,200*

Yes, many adjustments have to take place before what Accountants call a 'true and fair' picture emerges. Among these are depreciation of plant and machinery, maybe appreciation of buildings, and estimates of tax needing to be paid.

Cash Flow

What is of even more immediate importance is cash flow. As most accountants should tell you, your asset and equity position is unimportant if cash is flowing out of the business faster than it is coming in. To quote Mr Micawber in Charles Dicken's novel, "David Copperfield" - "Income of 20 shillings and expenditure of 19 shillings and six pence, result happiness; income of 20 shillings and expenditure of 20 shillings and sixpence, result misery".

So how do you know what your cash flow is over a period? Simple. Do a Trial Balance over that period.

Take for example the above Trial Balance.

TRIAL BALANCE
FRED'S MANUFACTURING LTD
As at 30 June 2012

NAME OF ACCOUNT	DEBIT BALANCES B/D	CREDIT BALANCES B/D
	$	$
Cash on Hand	*200*	
Stock at hand/inventory	*30,000*	
Plant and machinery	*100,000*	
Bank Loan overdraft/cash at bank		*20,000*
Buildings	*570,000*	
Accounts receivable	*20,000*	
Accounts payable		*10,000*
Shares nominal value		*100,000*
Accumulated capital		*524,300*
Sales Revenue		420,000
Discounts received		750
Rent Expense	750	
Raw material purchases	150,000	
Machinery purchases	50,000	
Wages and salaries	150,000	
Rates	1000	
Repairs	500	
Insurance	300	
Bank interest and charges	150	
Income Tax	400	
Postage	100	
Travel expenses	600	
Printing and stationary	400	
Discounts allowed	650	
TOTAL	1,075,050	1,075,050

Now, I refer back to the "Stocks" and "Flows" discussed at the beginning of the book. You are only interested in the Flows.

In the above Trial Balance the Stocks are shown in italics.

The Flows are not in italics, and can be divided into Income and Expenditure. Yes, we have the Revenue and Expenses statement above. But this can be over any period necessary.

Cash Flow

Account Name	DEBIT BALANCES B/D	CREDIT BALANCES B/D
	$	$
Revenue		
Sales		420,000
Discounts receive		750
Total revenue		*420,750*
Expenses		
Current expenses		
Rent expense	750	
Raw material purchases	150,000	
Wages and salaries	150,000	
Rates	1000	
Repairs	500	
Insurance	300	
Bank interest and charges	150	
Income Tax	400	
Postage	100	
Travel expenses	600	
Printing and stationary	400	
Discounts allowed	650	
Total current expenses	*304,350*	
Capital expenses		
Machinery purchases	50,000	
Total capital expenses	*50,000*	
Total expenses	*354,850*	
Net revenue		*65,900*

As can be seen in this case the total cash outflow over this period was $354,850 and total cash inflow was $420,750. The net positive difference was $65,900.

This is a net positive cash flow. Though net negative cash flows are certainly possible, they are certainly not desirable for any lengthy period. In fact, if you divide the value of the current assets by the value of the negative cash flow, you have a measure of how many days you have left to be solvent! As in Shakespeare's day, your demise could be soon, sudden and unexpected. So, watch your cash flow intensely. Other accounting information (including profits) is of a more theoretical nature. But cash flow has a direct effect on your survival. Frequent Trial Balances are a necessity for that reason alone!

The above result showing a positive cash flow would please Mr Micawber.

Frequency of Trial Balances

Many firms perform frequent Trial Balances – weekly or monthly. That's fine. I advise the more frequent the better. In today's world of electronic Bank Transfers I recommend having a weekly Trial Balance.

With a periodic Trial Balance you start with the balances at the end of the previous Trial Balance as the commencing balances for each account.

Now many want to do a Trial Balance of the entire year's transactions each time you do a Trail Balance, and not start at the Balance Brought Down at the end of the previous Trail Balance. How does one do that?

If you do a Trial Balance for an entire year's transactions you start each time with the starting balances for each account for that year.

Many accounting systems do not to have a physical "rule off" appearing on the page, but have a nominal rule off on a certain date, and estimate the balances for a certain period, from the beginning to the end of that period. The transactions keep accumulating on the ledger page without any ruling or notation. Each Trial Balance requires a separate set of computation, and it is of course open to error.

Many practical mechanical and computational methodologies have been devised for doing Trial Balances, and practical methodologies vary to some extent from firm to firm. The method I have described may probably look antiquated, but it is THE fundamental methodology. I warn that many 'short cuts' lead to problems. If you have any doubts at all, do the Trial Balance the way I have described.

Chapter 19

The vexed question of Capital

And now finally a couple of issues that are not directly related to learning bookkeeping, but are necessary to be aware of.

Many writers of business manuals try to confuse the poor student with the vexed question of Capital right at the start. These manual writers seem intent in getting the poor student into a knot right from the word go. But have you calmed down? You know what to do? Right. Well, Capital is a **Liability**. It is what your firm owes **you,** or the original investors. So, go up there and shove Capital into the Liabilities section of the Chart of Accounts.

You have to differentiate between the concept of Capital, and Cash and other Assets. Yes, originally Capital was also Cash. But that cash belonged to you or the investor. When you invested in the firm, the cash was placed in an account called Capital, and as the firm owes this cash to the investors it is a Liability for the firm.

Now an interesting question. Is it necessarily a good thing if a firm has a lot of Capital? For example, could you get a situation of a firm with a million dollars of Capital but not a cent in Assets?

Let's do an example of a hypothetical Memorandum.

Date	Description	Jnl no
1 July 2013	Million dollars of capital raised for ABC startup in form of $1 shares. Placed in bank a/c	1
2 July 2013	Million dollars paid in wages for services in startup	2

What does the journal look like?

First. There are two items, Cash at Bank, an Asset, and Capital, a Liability. Both are increased by one million dollars.

Increase an Asset. DEAr. Debit Cash at Bank.
Increase a Liability. CILla. Credit Capital.

JOURNAL (Example).

Date	Reference Number	Description	Debit	Credit
1 July 13	1	Cash at Bank	1,000,000	
1 July 13	1	Capital		1,000,000

Now the business spends all the Cash at Bank on wages!
Decrease an Asset. CEAr.
What about wages? You *increase* the amount sent on wages. An Expense. DEAr. Debit wages.

JOURNAL (Example).

Date	Reference Number	Description	Debit	Credit
1 July 13	1	Cash at Bank	1,000,000	
1 July 13	1	Capital		1,000,000
2 July 13	2	Wages	1,000,000	
2 July 13	2	Cash at Bank		1,000,000

You can immediately see that while Cash at Bank has been reduced to zero, Capital remains at one million dollars. The books still balance. Even though the amount spent on wages has presumably disappeared into the air, the books still say that the firm has a Capital of one million dollars.

As will be seen later, this paradox is dealt with in the Balance Sheet. The firm has a million dollars of Capital but no Assets. Its Liabilities are said to exceed it Assets by one million dollars.

It is worth remembering not to put too much weight on the stated Capital figure. It is of largely historical value, and appearances can and often try very much to deceive.

Chapter 20

Profits

and the

Cost of Goods Sold

Finally, there is the big question in estimating profits. Easy, you say. We have already discussed it. But oh no. Only half of it. The Trial Balance "profit", while very useful, has issues tied up with inventory valuation. This is not strictly a bookkeeping issue, but it governs the design and structure of your bookkeeping system. This is the grey area where accountants take over.

There is a big conundrum in bookkeeping lurking in the shadows – how do you account for changes in asset values? There are two separate accounting systems that operate in totally different ways for dealing with asset purchase and sales, including to and from inventories, and calculating profits.

I shall explain. Back in the days of Pacioli, there was no accounting distinction between 'Capital Stock' and 'Inventory'. So, when a merchant bought nutmegs, he debited the nutmegs account, and when he bought a ship, he debited the ship account. Both asset accounts. When he sold nutmegs, he credited the nutmegs account, and when he sold the ship he credited the ship account. When he wanted to calculate his profits he did a trial balance, and if he was in net credit he had made a profit. For accounting purposes, for calculating profits and losses, there was no distinction between selling nutmegs and selling the ship.

This happy state of affairs continued until the mid-nineteenth century. Then a big scandal occurred in Britain involving investing in railways, and Parliament specified that Capital Stock should be separated from the sale of Inventories and Services, and should be depreciated. Once this distinction had been made accountants worked out that you could also work out profits by using two new accounts, 'value of goods purchased', and 'value of goods sold'. Logical! But horrors! When you did that, you could not directly adjust asset values using double entry bookkeeping methods.

Huh! How is that?

So here is the reason from the start. When you are fully informed, you not only can but you must make a choice of what bookkeeping system to use. You cannot use both at the same time.

Is purchasing an Asset an Expense? Of course it is, you say.

But remember DEAr CILla (increase) and CEAr DILla (decrease).

You Debit the Asset to increase its value. DEAr.

You must Credit something. What?

If you Credit Expense CEAr you decrease it. **But** since you have added to (increased) Expenses you must increase it.

In other words, in Double Entry Bookeeping, *you cannot increase an Asset and an Expense at the same time.*

So, you can only Credit Liabilities (increase), ie borrow, or Credit Assets (decrease), by spending cash when you purchase an Asset.

You have a problem that has hit every bookkeeper since time immemorial, or at least since the nineteenth century. In the chapter above you just purchased $80 of supplies, and you Debited the supplies account, an asset account.

Yes, but what did I Credit? Another Asset account! Cash at Bank.

Let's take an example. You wish to add to your stock of Trophies. Debit it as you are increasing an asset. DEAr. You cannot use DEAr or DILla again. You must credit the account.

So CEAr or CILla. However, CEAr *decreases* the value of the expense and asset account. You need to *increase* the Expenses account.

CILla? Neither Income I or Liability L are expenses.

You have got yourself into a logical bind!

So, you cannot increase the Asset account and the Expense account simultaneously, as it would require two Debits. DEAr. Crediting won't increase an Expense account. CILla. You can only use DEAr CILla to increase accounts.

So when you want to purchase stocks, an asset, you cannot place the amount into an expense account to increase expenses, and thereby use the expenses to calculate profits by deducting expenses from sales.

Now we get to the more important issue. Suppose you had stocks or an inventory, from which you hope to sell from to make a profit.

Simple! Sell from an Asset. You reduce its value. CEAr. You must credit the inventory account.

Whoa! You must then Debit something. DEAr or DILla. But if you uses DILla you are decreasing an Income or Liability account. But you are trying to increase Income. And obviously you can't increase Expenses.

You cannot Sell an Asset and place the amount in a Sales account to increase sales value to calculate profits.

I know. You would just love to increase the Income account. But sorry. It can't be done. A logical bind.

Oh no! What do people doooo?

So, this is the conundrum. If you are selling from Inventory, you cannot account directly for the value of sales in an income account. If you are adding to Inventory, you cannot account directly for the value of purchases in an expense account, or as the accountants call it, Cost of Goods Sold.

With neither of these accounts being viable, you cannot account directly for Gross Profits (Value of sales less Cost of Goods Sold).

This was the state of play at the beginning of the Nineteenth century. But as the Industrial Revolution progressed the business people were not happy. The asset adjustment approach to calculating profit was insufficiently informative and detailed. Also including the sale of capital assets into profit (even though it is still used) was regarded as somewhat suspect. Profits were (and still are) intuitively seen as the result of short-term activities,

So, a work around was developed. It was raised by accountants to the status of THE methodology, but as will be shown, it is theoretically a bit suspect.

Basically, the accounting systems have been divided into two types. In the first, which I will call the Pacioli system (I will give it the accounting name shortly) the asset values are constantly adjusted by the buys and sales. At the end of the accounting period all, or most, of the asset accounting values are different.

Yes, there are Income and Expenses, but these only relate to transactions where the transaction is not acting directly on an Asset of Liability.

The net changes at the end of the period are estimated, and this gives the net profit. These net changes are estimated in terms of net Debits and Credits in a Trial Balance, which has been discussed. For a business of Pacioli's period, and centuries later, simple and satisfactory.

In the other methodology, *the asset values do not change at all in the accounts from beginning to the end of the period.* These values have to be adjusted by a separate methodology at the end of the period. (Or sometimes more frequently). On the other hand, there is a continuous update of the income and expenses accounts. Indeed, it became quickly apparent to certain early businessmen (such as Joshia Wedgewood – the manufacturer of china plates and cups) that the income from, and cost of, individual items could be recorded, and a continuous running sheet of gross profits, cost per item and so on could be maintained, when this "new" method of bookkeeping was used.

Thus, the business has a running account of the values of Supplies Purchased and Supplies Sold (or a similar nomenclature).

Accountants have an official name for the two methods for accounting for Inventories. These are:

1. The Perpetual Inventory Accounting System. This is the system I alluded to earlier as the 'Pacioli' system. All the asset movements, including inventory movements, are shown as they occur during the accounting period. Purchase and sales accounts are not used. Each time a purchase is made, the value of the purchase is recorded directly to the inventory account (a Debit). Similarly, each time a sale is made the value of the sale is recorded directly to the inventory account (a credit). While a net Credit figure does not directly show whether a gross profit is being made, a healthy credit in this account while the inventory is not falling shows that healthy profits are being made and accumulated.
2. The Periodic Inventory Accounting System. Running accounts of the values of the inventories purchased and inventories sold are used. The balance on the inventory asset account does *not* change through the accounting period, but remains at its opening balance until the end of the accounting period. At the end of the accounting period all the asset accounts need to be revalued. The capital accounts need to be depreciated (or occasionally appreciated). The inventory needs to counted and checked, and the balance adjusted to the physical count. Unlike the other system, there is nothing automatic about this process. The movement of inventory resulting from sale is not recorded in this system, and the cost of sales is calculated only at the end of the accounting system period using the formula:

Cost of sales = opening inventory + purchases – closing inventory.
Gross Profit = Total Revenue – Cost of Sales

So, which one should you use? For nearly one hundred years, the Periodic Inventory System was almost universally used. Cost of Sales, or Cost of Goods Sold as it is known, was ingrained into the accounting system.

As a practicing bookkeeper, if your firm uses the COGS system, you must resort to arbitrary "rules" to define the structure of your accounting system. While you will continue to use double entry, the Expense and Income accounts become more elaborate.

But there has now been a switch back by very large companies to the Perpetual Inventory System, largely because of the cost and trouble of revaluing inventories. For them, they have regular checks for stealing, deterioration and aging of stock, and a quick check of numbers. An adjustment of capital values is done at least annually, but the value of profits is not dependent on an estimated Cost of Goods Sold as previously calculated.

Which is best? My advice is leave it to the Accountant to make a choice. The arguments have swung back and forth with religious fervor, and unless you want to be involved in a Montague and Capulet battle (which it was in the accounting profession for a time) leave the matter to your betters. Or to the requirements of your company.

Nevertheless, now you know there is a fundamental accounting and logical reason for the two different bookkeeping systems, and they are not just a simple choice dreamt up by accountants.

Cost of Goods Sold

If you use the second method, the Periodic Inventory Accounting System, you hit a problem when you try to estimate Profits, and you need another measure to do this, the Cost of Goods Sold, or as it is known in accounting circles, COGS.

Gross Profit = Sales Revenue – Cost of Goods Sold

Net Profit = Net Sales – Cost of goods sold – operating expenses – taxes – interest

Now, in Double Entry Bookkeeping there is no automatic method of equating the actual cost of goods sold.

If you are a retailer, a method is to divide the goods purchased at any particular time by **the number of units purchased**, to get the value per unit.

Otherwise COGS is heavily tied up with inventory valuation, of which there are several methods allowed by accounting rules, plus others. All of which give a different answer, and a different net profit.

The following are used under the accounting rules in most countries:-

- Specific identification. Under this method, particular items are identified, and costs are tracked with respect to each item. This may require considerable recordkeeping. This method cannot be used where the goods or items are indistinguishable or fungible.
- Average cost. The average cost method relies on average unit cost to calculate cost of units sold and ending inventory. Several variations on the calculation may be used, including weighted average and moving average.
- First-In First-Out (FIFO) assumes that the items purchased or produced first are sold first. Costs of inventory per unit or item are determined at the time made or acquired. The oldest cost (*i.e.*, the first in) is then matched against revenue and assigned to cost of goods sold.
- Last-In First-Out (LIFO) is the reverse of FIFO. Some systems permit determining the costs of goods at the time acquired or made, but assigning costs to goods sold under the assumption that the goods made or acquired last are sold first.
- Retail inventory method. Resellers of goods may use this method to simplify recordkeeping. The calculated cost of goods on hand at the end of a period is the ratio of cost of goods acquired to the retail value of the goods times the retail value of goods on hand. Cost of goods acquired includes beginning inventory as previously valued plus purchases. Cost of goods sold is then beginning inventory plus purchases less the calculated cost of goods on hand at the end of the period.

In some cases, the cost of goods sold may be identified with the item sold. Ordinarily, however, the identity of goods is lost between the time of purchase or manufacture and the time of sale. Determining which goods have been sold, and the cost of those goods, requires either identifying the goods or using a convention to assume which goods were sold. This may be referred to as a cost flow assumption or inventory identification assumption or convention.

Yes. It is all very complicated. However, the point is, there is no specific account for the Cost of Goods Sold. The methodology requires drawing on the information from several accounts, and performing a process to find an estimate of the Cost of Goods Sold. This estimate is only approximate and depends on the purpose it is needed. There is no “true” accounting value for the Cost of Goods Sold.

This somewhat botched estimation of the profit figure is in my opinion the result of the use of the Periodic Inventory Accounting System instead of the Perpetual Inventory

Accounting System. A lot of ink has been spilt on this subject, but a choice has to be made. It is up to the firm's bosses to make this choice.

Chapter 21

Deriving Economic Rents

It is very simple to estimate the value of Economic Rents the firm is earning from this the Trial Balance Income Statement.

First, what are Economic Rents? I ask this question because very few people have heard of this concept, especially budding bookkeepers and accountants.

Economists, such as myself, laugh at the accounting concept of profit. They say that not only does this measure keep changing according to what accounting rules are applied: but, what is worse, the accounting concept of profit is fundamentally nonsense. What? Fundamentally nonsense! Yes. From the theoretical point of view there is no correct theoretical measure (that means having a correct mathematical proof) for whatever is the current measure for accounting profits, aside from the measure of economic rents. In other words, accountants cannot prove that their current measure of profit is theoretically correct!

The measure for accounting profits is based on a vague and erroneous arguments that divert the measure of accounting profits from this "true" measure of profits, economic rents. These erroneous arguments are based on a form of words that goes back to the mid 19th Century, that says that you must extract from revenue all variable costs but not expenditure on fixed costs. For this you only deduct "depreciation" (in inverted commas), but as a quid pro quo you add back any capital stock appreciation. Those are the basic aspirations. In actual practice the logic of this is so full of holes that tomes of "Accounting Rules" have grown up, many of them contradictory, and from an economist's point of view, do not make much sense. Yet Accountants have convinced everyone that this approach gives a "true and correct" measure of a firm's positions, and blindly follow these rules (although there is a wide variation in the level of interpretation!)

Needless to say, no investor with any sense believes either the published Profit and Loss Statements or Balance Sheets, and a whole industry has grown up delving into their mysteries. Successful analysts, such as Warren Buffet, have made fortunes doing this.

So, as most of the readers of this book have never heard of "Economic Rent", what is it?

What are Economic Rents? Economic Rents are also called Monopoly Profits, though that is not a complete description. While most non-economists instantly recognize what a Monopoly Profit is, and all Monopoly Profits are Economic Rents, there are many more examples of Economic Rents than there are of Monopoly Profits. Many Economic Rents are completely hidden, and have to be ferreted out.

The term "Economic Rents" is a confusing term because it has little to do with house rents or office rents per se. The term Rent is purely historic, and dates back to the writings of an early nineteenth century economist - David Ricardo. Ricardo was investigating the role of land rents and the influence they had on wheat prices, and showed that increasing land rents did not increase corn (wheat) prices. If a landowner increased his rents, the farmer could not increase the price of corn by "passing on" the rent increase. In the long term, as many 'squeezed' farmers got out, the only option for the landowner was to reduce his rents to allow the farmer to have a 'normal' profit.

If on the other hand when wheat prices increased, landowners could grab the entire increase in profit, leaving the farmer with just his normal profit. This is the situation that Henry George in his book "Progress and Poverty" railed against in the late 19th century. The owner of the land, whether rural or urban, obtained the entire economic rent increase, whether or not he had worked for it. Henry George went further and identified economic rents on both urban and rural land as the ultimate cause of poverty. All the workers' economic rents due to any increase in productivity were extracted for the ultimate benefit of the landowner, reducing the worker back to poverty.

Definition. Economic Rents are *the "excess returns" above the normal levels that are generated by competitive markets*. (Robert Tollinson, 1982, cited by Wikipedia). For our purposes this is one of the most useful definitions, one of scores of definitions cited by Wikipedia, as it ascribes "normal returns", and competition as part of the definition.

Normal returns or normal profits are the minimum level of profits caused by competition which allow a business to stay in business. In a competitive friction free economy, with no market failures, all business will operate under the same rate of profit, the normal profit. If any part of the economy has a higher rate of profit, competition will cause resources to shift to that part of the economy.

As you will immediately deduce, in the real world, above normal returns can and do occur, and continue to persist. In a real world economy, frictions and market failures are endemic, and cause firms to have a persistently high rate of profit, and indeed a low rate of profit that would cause firms eventually to exit from that industry.

So how do you measure economic rents?

Once in a while a totally obscure economics professor comes up with something earth-changing, a single written article, and he then falls back to obscurity. Sometimes they keep up the good work; but in the case of E Cary Brown they are rarely heard of again.

What did E Cary Brown do? In an obscure article (E. Cary Brown, 1948, "Business-Income taxation and Investment Incentives"), part of a compendium of articles in an obscure book written to celebrate the life of another economist (in l. Metter et al. "Income, Employment and Public Policy: Essays in Honor of Alvin H. Hansen", W.W. Norton, New York), E Cary Brown described a methodology to calculate the economic rent earned by a firm.

To cut to the chase, E. Cary Brown demonstrated that, in terms of a simple formula:

$$R = S - X - (C - I)$$

Where R is Economic Rent
S is Sales revenue
X is Capital Expenditure (yes, you deduct all 100% of it – there is NO deprecation of capital stock)
C is Current expenditure (as used by accountants as a deduction for accounting profits) and I is interest payments.

It is a very simple formula.

What this means that you deduct capital expenditure from revenue, deduct all other current expenditure from revenue (as in normal accounting procedures), except interest payments. This gives you the measure of economic rent.

This can be proven mathematically of course. There are numerous mathematical proofs available. A simple one is supplied by Boadway, R. W. and N. Bruce, 1979 "Depreciation and interest deductions and the effect on the corporation income tax on investment", Journal of Public Economics, pp. 93 -105.

Many accountants, business people and others trained in accounting get uncomfortable with the zero deduction for interest payments and the 100% deduction for capital expenditure, together with no depreciation deductions.

Live with it.

Yes, there are tax implications (called a tax on economic rents) but that won't be discussed here. If you are interested you can obtain another of my books called, yes, "Taxing Economic Rents", which will fill you in on this subject.

However, this economic rent can be very simply calculated from the Trial Balance. No capital "adjustments" needed.

Let's do it, with the above example. Assume that this Trial Balance is for the entire financial year – otherwise the rent and ratios you calculate would have to be multiplied pro rata.

Sales revenue S = $420,750

Capital expenditure X = $50,000

Current expenditure C = $304,350

Interest payments I = $150

Therefore using the formula

$R = S - X - (C - I)$

Economic rent R = $420,750 - $50,000 – ($304,350 - $150)

= $66,550

This is not a very useful figure unless it can be compared to something, such as the accounting measure of the firm's profits. (The above estimated Net Revenue is $65,900).

But a more useful measure is the return on assets, or alternatively the return on equity, both of these figures that can be obtained from the above balance sheet.

The return on assets $= \frac{\$66,550}{\$720,200}$

= 9.2% per annum

Not a bad return on assets.

The return on equity $= \frac{\$66,550}{\$690,200}$

= 9.6% per annum

Again, not a bad return on equity.

So, you can see that the Trial Balance gives you a very quick and easy measure of how the firm is performing. It is also argued by curmudiongly economists such as myself that it gives a better measure of profits than the "true and fair" measure estimated by accountants.

And Economic Rents can be directly and quickly estimated from a Trial Balance!

Conclusion

This book has taken you step by step, teaching you how to do Double Entry Bookkeeping, starting at listing the plethora of transactions right at the start in a Memorandum to deriving a Profit and Loss Statement and Balance sheet from the Trial Balance at the end.

The process is as follows:

1. List all the transactions in detail, big or small, buy or sell, in date order as they occur. The need to carry out this first step is emphasized, and neglecting it will lead to certain loss. This list can be entered from the transaction receipts and written evidence such as invoices, or from electronic records. There are a variety of names for this list; among them, “Memorandum” or “Day Book”.
2. The next stage is completing the Journal using the information derived from the abovementioned “Memorandum”. The Journal has two columns, the Debit column and the Credit column. Every transaction is entered into both the Debit and Credit column at the same time. There are also two other columns, one for the transaction number, and the other for the two account names that accompany each transaction.
3. All transactions are divided into four categories: Asset, Liability, Income and Expense.
4. Instructions on how to complete the Journal are discussed. We now introduce the mnemonics DEAR CILLA and CEAR DILLA. The mnemonic DEAR CILLA is used when you are *increasing* the value of an account. CEAR DILLA is used when you are *decreasing* the value of an account. D means place the transaction in the *Debit* column. C means place the transaction in the *Credit* column. E means that the transaction is an *Expense*, A means the transaction is an *Asset*, I means the transaction is *Income*, L means the transaction is a *Liability*.
5. We next come to the Ledger. The Ledger is a separate account book, and every account has a separate page. The Ledger also has an index locating the page number of every account.
6. Each page of the Ledger has an account name at its head, a column for the journal number, a column for the name of the corresponding account, and two columns, one for Debits, and one for Credits.
7. For every transaction, *two entries are made – double entry*, on two separate account pages. Guidance is taken from the Journal entry. Where the transaction says Debit for a particular account, place the amount in the Debit column on that Account page. Where the transaction says Credit, place the amount in the

Credit column on that Account page. In the Account Name column place the name of the corresponding account. Place the Journal Number of that transaction in the Journal Number account. Do this for all transactions as they occur.

8. The above is the process of Double Entry. Then we come to two "end of period" process – Bank Reconciliation, and Trial Balance. Both are checks on the accuracy of the process.
9. Bank Reconciliation is the process that checks to assure you that the accounting Cash at Bank balance is the same as the value of Cash at Bank, after making adjustments, mainly for flows of cash which have not yet been recorded in the Bank. The chapter on Bank Reconciliation goes into this in detail. It is not a complex process if it is taken step by step.
10. To obtain a Trial Balance it is necessary to "Rule Off" all the accounts at a certain date. Then a net balance is obtained, as the difference between the smallest credit or debit total and the largest. This is called the 'Balance Carried Down'. Then this Balance Carried Down is transferred to the opposite column and called the 'Balance Brought Down'.
11. To create a Trial Balance you use a form with a Debit and a Credit column, and a column for the account names. All the Balances Brought Down are listed as Debits or Credits on this Trial Balance form with their respective account names. If the Trial Balance is correct the Debit and Credit columns should have equal totals. If not, there are procedures to track down the error.
12. Finally a Profit and Loss Statement and Balance Sheet can be obtained from the Trial Balance. Arrange the contents of the Trial Balance so that all the 'flow' items are together, and all the 'stock' items are together. Then identify the stocks and flows separately – different colors or italics.
13. Take the flow items separately, and place the figures in a Profit and Loss Statement. The totals do not balance. The net difference should be added to one side or the other as a Profit or a Loss.
14. Take all the stock figures and arrange them in a Balance Sheet. If the Profit or Loss obtained from the Profit and Loss Statement is added to or subtracted from the Equity section the Balance Sheet should balance.
15. The very important cash flow figure can be derived from the Trial Balance. That alone, if done frequently, it is not only a useful reason, but also a vital reason, for carrying out frequent Trial Balances.
16. That is the end of the bookkeeping process. From here on accountant's step in to make the accounting 'adjustments' to produce the accounting Profit and Loss and Balance Sheet.

An Addendum was added to this book showing how an estimate of the Economic Rent earned by the firm could be calculated. For any bookkeeper or businessperson, that alone is worth the value of the book!

It is true that this book has avoided discussing many of the detailed requirements of bookkeeping, such as accrual accounting, cash and sales journals, credit sales and purchase accounts, treatment of bills of exchange, and much of the detailed day to day requirements of bookkeeping in an average medium sized firm. To do that the book would have needed to be much larger. The purpose of the book is to instill the basics of double entry bookkeeping into the reader, remove the confusion, and remove the need for a diktat from the Accountant on what to do. You can work it out for yourself from first principles. I might add that there is no standard bookkeeping system, aside from the theory discussed in this book, and it varies considerably from firm to firm. Learning that you must use a cash journal, say, may set you up for a shock in your first job when you find that the firm uses something different.

I might add that I do not approve of accrual accounting. While the stated purpose of accrual accounting is to record revenues when expenses are expected to occur, not when cash is exchanged; the practical effect due to the large amount of judgement involved has been to introduce excessive error and bias into the accounting results. This has led to (guess what?), many instances where dishonest companies have published very false results, bringing into the current accounts expected revenues that did not materialize. To quote Professor James Spellman of George Washington University Graduate School of Political Management, "(using accrual accounting).. CFO's are able to inflate income, grow receivables faster than sales, and keep the books open beyond a fiscal year's last day to surreptitiously capture more revenue". In other words, with accrual accounting, there is excessive reliance on the honesty and professional competence of the accountant. The experience over even hundreds of years is that this is not a good idea.

I hope that you enjoyed reading the book, and more importantly, that you have *learned* to *do* Double Entry Bookkeeping. It is an invaluable skill. From now on, if you apply this knowledge no one can cheat you. You will always know how much you owe and how much you are worth at any point in time, and whether you are cash flow positive. A working knowledge of Double Entry Bookkeeping is one of the most valuable assets you will ever acquire.

Finally, I can hear the words "It is all handled by computers. What does it matter?" If you do not understand what the computer should be doing, and you are not capable of checking the process step by step against double entry requirements, you are certain to be swindled. Learn and understand the fundamentals of Double Entry Bookkeeping.

Printed in Great Britain
by Amazon

67920779R00079